Of all the things a wife can do for her husband, or all the many ways she can show her support, nothing tops the prayers she offers up before the Throne. And it's the wise wife who, when she prays, recognizes how her marriage—even her own life—is being strengthened and deepened. God sees when women kneel in prayer for their husbands, and *Prayers of an Excellent Wife* provides the reader with all the scriptural principles and language needed to cover a man with powerful intercession—prayers so effective, they'll resonate throughout his life."

> —JONI EARECKSON TADA
> Joni and Friends International Disability Center

Just imagine how our marriages, families and in turn the cause of Christ would be forever changed if godly wives took seriously their responsibility to pray for their husbands. We know that we are commanded to pray—and to pray daily and specifically for our husbands. Sadly, that mandate too often gets pushed aside, to Satan's delight and our detriment, by the hectic pace of our lives. *Prayers of An Excellent Wife* provides a template that if used properly will indeed produce excellent wives who faithfully and passionately pray God's word for their precious husbands. Andrew Case has skillfully compiled scores of poignant scriptural passages that when raised to God's ear by the sincerity of a praying wife will move mountains. I encourage Christian women everywhere to embrace this privilege that is ours to pray. I recommend this book as an excellent resource to intentionally do so. May we never underestimate how God will use our earnest prayers to raise up husbands who will lovingly lead their wives and families; who will be emboldened for the arduous work of the Kingdom, and who will eagerly seek to glorify the name of Christ alone.

> —MARY K. MOHLER
> Wife of R. Albert Mohler, Jr.
> Director of Seminary Wives Institute,
> The Southern Baptist Theological Seminary

Charles Spurgeon said we can do our husband "no truer kindness in the world" than to pray for him. Yet as wives, we often struggle to pray consistently for our husbands. We forget in the busyness of life; or when we do remember, our prayers may lack clarity and direction. That's what makes this book such a valuable tool for any wife who wants to grow in praying for her husband—and isn't that all of us? *Prayers of an Excellent Wife* will inspire you to pray faithfully and fervently, and instruct you how to pray according to Scripture. I hope many wives will use these prayers to lavish their husbands with kindness.

> —CAROLYN MAHANEY
> Author of *Feminine Appeal*

What better words to pray for our husbands than the very words of his Maker? *Prayers of an Excellent Wife* provides a guide for humbly engaging in the joyful duty of intercession, petition and thanksgiving for our husbands. I am delighted to speak these prayers with and on behalf of Matt.

—LAUREN CHANDLER
Wife of Matt Chandler who is preaching pastor at The Village Church, Highland Village, TX

My prayers for Tom can become tepid and redundant. This book personalizes Scripture into prayers, touching on areas that I don't always think of to pray for him. The quotes sprinkled throughout are very insightful as well. I would recommend it to any wife who is wanting to deepen and expand her prayer life for her husband. It only takes a few minutes so it's easy to incorporate into one's devotional time.

—DIANE SCHREINER

What an excellent gift Andrew Case has given us in *Prayers of an Excellent Wife*. He uses biblical passages and truths as springboards for thoughtful, faithful prayers that wives can pray for and with their husbands. I have told wives many times that one of the best ways to help our husbands is to pray for them. Here are many beautiful, poetic prayers that can help us do so. May God be pleased to use this tool to further His sanctifying work in the lives of many husbands and wives.

—JODI WARE
Wife, Mother, Homemaker
Seminary Wives Institute Instructor
The Southern Baptist Theological Seminary

My friend Andrew instructs us to persevere in this 'loving labor' of prayer for our husbands, and has graciously provided the perfect tool to assist us on our journey. What a gift God has given Andrew in skillfully weaving the beauty and wisdom of scripture with heartfelt prayer. I wholeheartedly commend this thoughtful book to every wife who earnestly desires to do good to her husband all the days of her life. May God use this rich resource to cultivate Christ-centered marriages that glorify Him!

—AMY WILLIAMS

for
my dear father and mother
who have shown me what it looks like
to be ever faithful in prayer

Andrew Case, *Prayers of an Excellent Wife*

Edited by Joy Hernandez

ISBN 978-14-4953-4028

Prayers of an Excellent Wife

She does him good, and not harm,
all the days of her life.
~ Proverbs 31:12

Contents

Preface

She Does Him Good, and Not Harm

In the beginning God created the heavens and the earth. And He made everything in the heavens and on the earth. And God saw that it was good. All of it. Except one thing: "The LORD God said, 'It is *not good* that man should be alone'" (Gen 2:18). This staggering declaration has never stopped resounding throughout history as man senses again and again his keen need of a "helper fit for him." And she is indeed fit for him, having been built from his own body to build him up.

The primeval story of her creation is nearly too good to be true. As Martin Luther comments, "Perhaps no one would believe the account of how Eve was created, were it not clearly taught in Scripture."[1] The account reads as follows:

> Now out of the ground the LORD God had formed every beast of the field and every bird of the heavens and brought them to the man to see what he would call them. And whatever the man called every living creature, that was its name. The man gave names to all livestock and to the birds of the heavens and to every beast of the field.
> But for Adam there was not found a helper fit for him. So the LORD God caused a deep sleep to fall upon the man, and while he slept took one of his ribs and closed up its place with flesh. And the rib that the LORD God had taken from the man he made into a woman and brought her to the man. Then the man said, "This at last is bone of my bones and flesh of my flesh; she shall be called Woman, because she was taken out of Man." Therefore a man shall leave his father and his mother and hold fast to his wife, and they shall become one

---

[1] Martin Luther, *Luther's Commentary On Genesis*, trans. J. Theodore Mueller, vol. 1 (Zondervan: Grand Rapids, 1958), 58.

flesh. And the man and his wife were both naked and were not ashamed. (Gen 2:19-25)

There is a beautiful, purposeful meaning to be seen in how God brings her into being. The story has a "poetic flavor" that leads to the outburst of poetry from the man. In an attempt to bring out some of this meaning and flavor, Matthew Henry comments that the woman was "not made out of [the man's] head to top him, not out of his feet to be trampled upon by him, but out of his side to be equal with him, under his arm to be protected, and near his heart to be beloved."[2]

Under divinely induced sleep, a rib is taken out of the man. This should not be seen merely as a surgical operation, but as a brilliant depiction of the relationship between a man and his wife. She is intricately woven out of his very substance, one flesh with him, ontologically bound to him as the helper who stands always at his side. Calvin observes that something was taken from the man

> in order that he might embrace, with greater benevolence, a part of himself. He lost, therefore, one of his ribs; but, instead of it, a far richer reward was granted him, since he obtained a faithful associate of life; for he now saw himself, who had before been imperfect, rendered complete in his wife.[3]

God deliberately did not form her out of the dust from the ground, but instead built her from the man's living, organized substance. Neither did God create her out of nothing. Thus, among all the living creatures, woman remains entirely unique in her origin and at the same time inextricably linked

---

[2]M. Henry, *A Commentary on the Holy Bible* (London: Marshall Brother, n.d.), 1:12.

[3]John Calvin, *Commentaries on Genesis*, trans. John King, vol. 1 (Grand Rapids: Baker, n.d.), 133.

to the man, deriving her spiritual and material nature from him.[4]

A theology of headship is portrayed beautifully by the depiction of the woman being built from the man. In his letter to the Corinthians the Apostle Paul references this account to make a point: "For man was not made from woman, but woman from man. Neither was man created for woman, but woman for man" (I Cor 11:8-9). Previously in the same chapter Paul has just said that "the head of a wife is her husband" (I Cor 11:3), to which he now adds primordial support.

The implications of woman's origin are profound. Her dignity and worth, her necessity, her role in life and marriage, and her unique beauty have been established by God from the beginning. She was made to be a man's faithful helper. And there is no greater help she can offer him than her prayers on his behalf to the One who alone can provide perfect, sovereign help. When the psalmist sings, "I lift my eyes to the hills. From where does my *help* come?" he answers his own question with the words, "My help comes *from the* LORD who made heaven and earth." You are not sufficient succor for him. A stronger Hand must come to his aid. Blessed is the wife who pleads often for this mighty Hand to keep her husband's life; who begs for him at the gates of Grace. This is the sort of woman who fears the LORD, feels her own weakness, and finds refuge and righteousness in Jesus Christ. She wants *God* for her husband. She is to be praised.

---

[4]Franz Delitzsch, *A New Commentary On Genesis*, trans. Sophia Taylor, vol. 1 (Edinburgh: T. & T. Clark, 1888), 142.

If you want to be an excellent wife, far more precious than jewels, pray for your husband. If you want to do him good, and not harm, all the days of your life, pray for him. If you desire to be a wife whose husband is "known in the gates when he sits among the elders of the land," pray for him. If you open your mouth with wisdom, may it be full of wise prayers for your husband. Let not charm or fleeting beauty distract you from this vital task. The fruit of wise prayers will be better for him than the fruit of your hands. When it comes to this loving labor, may you never be found eating the bread of idleness.

You have submitted yourself to the leadership of a mortal man with a sinful heart, therefore intercede all the more for him. He is your head, but his head is Christ, and the head of Christ is God (I Cor 11:3), and you have been given privileged access to Him through Jesus. Therefore never tire in lifting your husband up to God to be led in righteousness so that he might turn and lead you in the same. And when you do pray, use God's Word. O what a treasure trove of prayer is afforded to us in the Bible! Seize its wisdom of petition and exultation, and learn to be a conduit of its perfect intercession, entrusting your husband to his Maker, the Supreme Ruler of all the world.

Not until after ten years of wavering prayers did George Mueller learn the value of praying Scripture. What follows is his description of this marvelous discovery.

> The difference then between my former practice and my present one is this. Formerly, when I arose, I began to pray as soon as possible.... But what was the result? I often spent a quarter of an hour, or half an hour, or even an hour on my knees before being conscious to myself of having derived comfort, encouragement, humbling of soul, &c.; and often, after having suffered much

from wandering of mind for the first ten minutes, or a quarter of an hour, or even half an hour, I only then began *really to pray*. I scarcely ever suffer now in this way.

My practice had been, at least for ten years previously, as an habitual thing, to give myself to prayer, after having dressed myself in the morning. *Now...*the first thing I did, after having asked in a few words the Lord's blessing upon His precious word, was, to begin to meditate on the word of God, searching, as it were, into every verse, to get blessing out of it.... The result I have found to be almost invariably this, that after a very few minutes my soul has been led to confession, or to thanksgiving, or to intercession, or to supplication; so that, though I did not, as it were, give myself to *prayer*, but to *meditation*, yet it turned almost immediately more or less into prayer. When thus I have been for awhile making confession, or intercession, or supplication, or have given thanks, I go on to the next words or verse, turning all, as I go on, into prayer for myself or others, as the Word may lead to it.[5]

This book is meant to be a help and guide for that kind of praying. It consists of little else than the Word of God turned "more or less into prayer." And more specifically it is a means toward one part of prayer—prayer for the husband God has given you. We would do well to heed the council of Thomas Manton: "plead the promise of God in prayer, show Him His handwriting; God is tender of His Word." Many women have done excellently in this, but may you surpass them all.

---

[5]George Mueller, *A Narrative of Some of the Lord's Dealing with George Mueller, Written by Himself, Jehovah Magnified. Addresses by George Mueller Complete and Unabridged,* 2 vols. (Muskegon, Mich.: Dust and Ashes Publications, 2003), 1:272-273.

Instructions to the Reader

Make It Your Own

Jesus Christ is emphatically the foundation for every prayer to the Father. But the reader will notice that not all of these prayers put this precious truth into words, simply because they are meant to be springboards that launch us into other specific and more personal prayer. You are encouraged to use them as a means of centering your mind on the Bible, so that what follows in your own individual supplications will be sweetened and guided by the Word and Spirit of God.

Therefore many times I have left it to you, the reader, to be mindful that we pray in Christ's name alone. Indeed, as He Himself said, "No one comes to the Father except through me" (John 14:6). Thus we are to come to the Father in prayer always through Christ and only through Christ. Only because He is our Great High Priest can we "with confidence draw near to the throne of grace, that we may receive mercy and find grace to help in time of need" (Heb 4:16). And we are to give "thanks always and for everything to God the Father *in the name of our Lord Jesus Christ*" (Eph 5:20).

These prayers are also not intended to be merely read alone. To the married woman I commend frequent use of these prayers *with* her husband, praying them over him from her heart, using his name. This should be the rule and not the exception, so that he is regularly reminded that his wife loves and respects him, and that the Word of God abounds with sanctifying power. For this reason a short exhortation or encouragement for him is included in many of the prayers, usually beginning with "O beloved...." Take these as occasions to lift his spirit, to strengthen his soul, to sharpen his mind, to gladden his heart, to put a rock of confidence under his feet, to tenderly and humbly correct, and most of all, to point him to God as his all-satisfying joy.

As with all prayer, these must be employed in a spirit of humility, considering him better and more significant than yourself (Phil 2:3). Be ever conscious of your broken condition—that you are a sinful woman who is in need of continual renewal by which you are being conformed to the image of Christ (Rom 8:29). Therefore pray strongly, as one who knows she is weak. Pray boldly, as one who knows she has no ability or confidence of herself. Pray sweetly, as one well aware of the heart within her still tinged with the bitter fruit of wickedness. And pray mindful of the truth that you are in need of just as much intercession as he. "This is the one to whom I will look: he who is humble and contrite in spirit and trembles at My word" (Isa 66:2).

Finally, I solemnly charge you before the God and Father of our Lord Jesus Christ to never neglect the joy and privilege of interceding for your husband. Do him good and not harm, all the days of your life. Help him by appealing to the Sovereign Helper. Whatever you do for him, do not fail or forget to do the best thing. He is a gift too wonderful for you to care for alone; Sovereign Grace must guard, guide, and govern his heart and life.

Be encouraged, dear Christian reader, with fresh earnestness to give yourself to prayer, if you can only be sure that you ask for things which are for the glory of God.
~George Mueller

Prayer, at its best, is the noblest, the sublimest, the most magnificent, and stupendous act that any creature of God can perform on earth or in heaven. Prayer is far too princely a life for most men. It is high, and they are low, and they cannot attain it.
~Alexander Whyte

Keeper of Your elect, It is better to take refuge in You than to trust in man. It is better to take refuge in You than to trust in princes. Therefore cause my husband to take refuge in You alone. Be his strength and his song; be his great salvation.

Let him lift up the cup of salvation and call on Your Name. Open to him the gates of righteousness, that he may enter through them and give thanks to You. Raise his eyes to the hills to see from where his help comes. For his help comes from You, who made heaven and earth. Do not let his foot be moved; keep him and do not slumber. Please keep him and neither slumber nor sleep. Keep him from all evil; keep his life. Keep his going out and his coming in from this time forth and forevermore.

My beloved, do you know who keeps you? The LORD is your keeper, the LORD is your shade on your right hand. The sun shall not strike you by day, nor the moon by night.

LORD, keep my husband. We wait eagerly for Your Son's appearing. Hasten the wonderful day of His return—the wedding supper of the Lamb. Amen (Psalm 118, 116, 121).

Precious Provider,

Your testimonies are wonderful; therefore my soul keeps them. May my husband keep them also. The unfolding of Your word gives light; it imparts understanding to the simple. May he open his mouth and pant, because he longs for Your commandments. Turn to him and be gracious to him, as is Your way with those who love Your name.

Keep steady his steps according to Your promise, let no iniquity get dominion over him. Redeem him from man's oppression, that he may keep Your precepts. Make Your face shine upon him, Your faithful servant, and teach him Your statutes. May his eyes shed streams of tears, because people do not keep Your law (Psalm 119).

A man cannot live unless he takes his breath, nor can the soul, unless it breathes forth its desires to God. ~Thomas Watson

LORD God of heaven,
The great and awesome God who keeps covenant and steadfast love with those who love Him and keep His commandments, let Your ear be attentive and Your eyes open, to hear the prayer of Your servant that I now pray before You day and night for my husband. Grant him continual patience and forbearance to live with me, a wicked wife. For I have sinned against You; I have acted very corruptly against You by forsaking my duty to help my husband lead our home in righteousness and the fear of You; I have not kept Your commandments, Your statutes, or the rules that You commanded Your servant Moses.

Give him boldness and wisdom to rebuke and exhort me when I am unfaithful to Your Word, when I neglect prayer, fail to redeem the time, speak carelessly, walk foolishly, fail to hope in You, seek great things for myself, become anxious about tomorrow. Do not let him cease praying for me when I am beset with the fear of man, the cares of the world, or the love of money. May he never lose confidence that, in spite of my many iniquities and shortcomings, I am Your servant whom You have redeemed by Your great power and by Your strong hand.

O Lord, let Your ear be attentive to the prayer of Your servant, and to the prayers of my husband who delights to fear Your name, and give success to him today, and grant him mercy (Nehemiah 1).

Merciful Master,
Look on his affliction and deliver him, and let him not forget Your law. Plead his cause and redeem him; give him life according to Your promise! Salvation is far from the wicked, for they do not seek Your statutes. Great is Your mercy, O LORD; give him life according to Your rules.

Even when his persecutors and adversaries are many, let him not swerve from Your testimonies. May he look at the faithless with pity, because they do not keep Your commands. Consider how he loves Your precepts! Give him life according to Your steadfast love. The sum of Your word is truth, and every one of Your righteous rules endures forever (Psalm 119).

To begin the day with prayer is but a formality unless it go on in prayer, unless for the rest of it we pray in deed what we began in word. One has said that while prayer is the day's best beginning it must not be like the handsome title-page of a worthless book. ~ P. T. Forsyth

overeign Preserver,

Let my dear husband stand up and bless You our God from everlasting to everlasting. Blessed be Your glorious name, which is exalted above all blessing and praise. You are the LORD, You alone. You have made *him.* You have made heaven, the heaven of heavens, with all their host, the earth and all that is on it, the seas and all that is in them; and You preserve all of them; and the host of heaven worships You.

Thank You for preserving my husband, for keeping him as Your chosen, for directing his steps on the narrow way. Please continue to preserve his life! For You are the LORD, the God who chose him and brought him out of darkness and made his heart faithful before You. Thank You that You have kept the promises that are his in Christ Jesus, for You are righteous. I praise You that You are a God ready to forgive, gracious and merciful, slow to anger and abounding in steadfast love, and have not departed from him. Even when he strays and his heart grows dull, You in Your great mercies have not forsaken him. Therefore, keep on making a name for Yourself through him, and instruct him with Your good Spirit. Amen (Nehemiah 9).

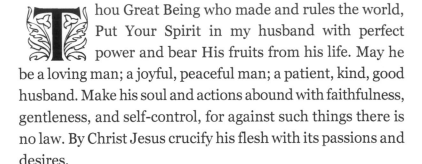 hou Great Being who made and rules the world, Put Your Spirit in my husband with perfect power and bear His fruits from his life. May he be a loving man; a joyful, peaceful man; a patient, kind, good husband. Make his soul and actions abound with faithfulness, gentleness, and self-control, for against such things there is no law. By Christ Jesus crucify his flesh with its passions and desires.

Let him not grow weary in doing good, for in due season he will reap if he does not give up. And may he never boast except in the cross of our Lord Jesus Christ, by which the world has been crucified to him, and he to the world (Galatians 5 & 6).

Prayer seem'd to be natural to me; as the breath, by which the inward burnings of my heart had vent. ~Jonathan Edwards

reat God,

      May my husband be a man inclined to pour himself out for the hungry and satisfy the desire of the afflicted, so that his light will rise in the darkness and his gloom be as the noonday. Then guide him continually and satisfy his desire in scorched places. Make his bones strong, so that he is like a watered garden, like a spring of water, whose waters do not fail.

May he be radiant; his heart thrilled to say, "I will greatly rejoice in the LORD; my soul shall exult in my God, for He has clothed me with the garments of salvation; He has covered me with the robe of righteousness." Make him count the garments of salvation as sufficient clothing, valued by him as more precious and worthy of care than the adornments of a king. May his robes of righteousness be ever prevalent, outshining worldly dress. Amen (Isaiah 58 & 61).

Righteous are You, O LORD, and right are Your rules. You have appointed Your testimonies in righteousness and in faithfulness. May zeal consume my husband when his foes forget Your words. Your promise is well tried; may he love it. Even when he is small and despised, let him not forget Your precepts. Your righteousness is righteous forever, and Your law is true. When trouble and anguish find him out, make Your commandments his delight. Your testimonies are righteous forever; give him understanding that he may live.

With my whole heart I cry for him; answer me, O LORD! Cause him to keep Your statutes. I call to You; save him, that he may observe Your testimonies. I rise before dawn and cry for help; may he hope in Your words. Awaken his eyes before the watches of the night, that he may meditate on Your promise. Hear my voice according to Your steadfast love; O LORD, according to Your justice give him life. When they draw near who persecute him with evil purpose, who are far from Your law, assure him that You are near, O LORD, and all Your commandments are true. Long have I known from Your testimonies that You have founded them forever (Psalm 119).

What makes a heart upright and what makes prayers pleasing to God is a felt awareness of our tremendous need for mercy.
~John Piper

My Gracious Master, Cause my husband to work out his own salvation with fear and trembling, knowing all the while that it is You who work in him, both to will and to work for Your good pleasure.

May he rejoice in You always, and let his reasonableness be known to everyone. Please let him not be anxious about anything, but in everything by prayer and supplication with thanksgiving may he make known his requests to You. And all this so that Your peace, which surpasses all understanding, will guard his heart and mind in Christ Jesus.

Finally Father, make him think on whatever is true, whatever is honorable, whatever is just, whatever is pure, whatever is lovely, whatever is commendable, on anything of excellence, and anything worthy of praise. Through Your Son and for Your glory I ask these things. Amen (Philippians 2 & 4).

Couples who do not pray are as badly off as those who stop sleeping together. Like lovemaking, prayer requires, in a sense, taking off the clothes, removing the shoes to touch holy ground.
~Mike Mason

eavenly Father,

As for me, my prayer is to You. At an acceptable time, O God, in the abundance of Your steadfast love answer me in Your saving faithfulness. And my prayer is this: deliver my husband from sinking in the mire of sin; let him be delivered from the deep waters of vanity. Let not the flood sweep over him, or the deep swallow him up, or the pit of despair close its mouth over him. Answer me, O LORD, for Your steadfast love is good; according to Your abundant mercy turn to him. Draw near to his soul, redeem him; ransom him because of his frailty.

When he is afflicted and in pain, let Your salvation, O God, set him on high! Then may he praise Your Name with a song, and magnify You with thanksgiving. May he seek You, and rejoice and be glad in You!

O beloved, because we love His salvation, let us say together evermore, "God is great!" Hasten to us, O God! You are our help and our deliverer; O LORD, do not delay! Save us for Your marvelous Name (Psalm 69 & 70).

Blessed God,
Although princes may persecute him without cause, may my husband's heart stand in awe of Your words. Might he, by the power of Your Spirit, rejoice at Your word like one who finds great spoil. Make him hate and abhor falsehood, but love Your law. Cause him to praise You seven times a day for Your righteous rules. Great peace have those who love Your law; nothing can make them stumble. May he hope for Your salvation, O LORD, and do Your commandments. Cause his soul to keep Your testimonies and love them exceedingly. Help him to keep Your precepts and testimonies, for all his ways are before You.

Let my cry come before You, O LORD; give him understanding according to Your word! Let my plea come before You; deliver him according to Your word. May his lips pour forth praise, for You teach him Your statutes. May his tongue sing of Your word, for all Your commandments are right. Let Your hand be ready to help him, for he has chosen Your precepts. Create in him a longing for Your salvation, O LORD, and a delight in Your law. Let his soul live and praise You, and let Your rules help him. When he goes astray like a lost sheep, seek him, Your servant, for he does not forget Your commandments. Amen (Psalm 119).

You often feel that your prayers scarcely reach the ceiling; but, oh, get into this humble spirit by considering how good the Lord is, and how evil you all are, and then prayer will mount on wings of faith to heaven. The sigh, the groan of a broken heart, will soon go through the ceiling up to heaven, aye, into the very bosom of God. ~Charles Simeon

Even skeptical Dan prayed, his skepticism falling away from him like a discarded garment in this valley of the shadow, which sifts out hearts and tries souls, until we all, grown-up or children, realize our weakness, and, finding that our own puny strength is as a reed shaken in the wind, creep back humbly to the God we have vainly dreamed we could do without.
~L.M. Montgomery

ord Jesus,
It is by Your undying death and willing sacrifice that I come to my Father who has loved me with an everlasting love for no reason but His own purpose and glory. And so I ask, LORD and Sovereign, that my husband would be blessed because his way is blameless; that he would walk in the law of the LORD! Cause him to keep Your testimonies and seek You with his whole heart, doing no wrong but walking in Your ways.

May he keep Your precepts diligently for love of Your great Name. Oh, that his ways may be steadfast in keeping Your statutes! May his blessed eyes be fixed unswervingly on all Your commandments. Please ignite such joy in him that he must praise You with an upright heart when he learns Your righteous rules. And cause him to keep Your statutes; do not utterly forsake him!

Keep his way pure by teaching him to guard it according to Your word. I ask that he be made into such a man who seeks You with his whole heart, crying out, "Let me not wander from Your commandments." May he store up Your word in his heart that he might not sin against You. Blessed are You, O LORD; teach him Your statutes!

May his lips be not only consecrated to me, but all the more to declaring the rules of Your mouth. And with all my might I plead that in the way of Your testimonies he would delight as much as in all riches...as much as in all friends...more so than any worldly lust and pleasure. Quicken his mind to meditate on Your precepts and fix his eyes on Your ways. I desire little else for him than that he delight in Your statutes and not forget Your word (Psalm 119).

Ineffable Lover,

Only by the Cross do I bring these prayers to You. For my husband's sake, let me not be a woman whose adorning is merely external—the braiding of hair, the wearing of gold, or the putting on of clothing—but make my adorning be the hidden person of the heart with the imperishable beauty of a gentle and quiet spirit, which in Your sight is very precious.

Give him unity of mind, sympathy, brotherly love, a tender heart, and humility. The end of all things is at hand; therefore let him be self-controlled and sober-minded for the sake of his prayers. Above all, keep him loving others earnestly, since love covers a multitude of sins.

As he has received a gift, may he use it to serve others, as a good steward of Your varied grace. When he speaks, let it be as one who speaks the oracles of God; when he serves, as one who serves by the strength that You supply—in order that in everything You may be glorified through Jesus Christ. To You belong glory and dominion forever and ever. Amen (I Peter 3 & 4).

How much my father's prayers at this time impressed me I can never explain, nor could any stranger understand. When, on his knees and all of us kneeling around him in Family Worship, he poured out his whole soul with tears for the conversion of the Heathen world to the service of Jesus, and for every personal and domestic need, we all felt as if in the presence of the living Savior, and learned to know and love him as our Divine friend.
~James C. Paton

od of my end,
Deal bountifully with my husband, Your servant, that he may live and keep Your word. And this I ask with importunate reverence: open his eyes, that he may behold wondrous things out of Your law. O that his eyes would sparkle with pure and deep delight when Your Truth shines into them out of grace. For he is a mere sojourner on this earth; hide not Your commandments from him!

Consume his soul with longing for Your rules at all times, for You rebuke the insolent, accursed ones, who wander from Your commandments. Take away from him scorn and contempt, for he has kept Your testimonies. Cause him to meditate on Your statutes even when princes sit plotting against him. May this be readily on his lips: "Your testimonies are my delight; they are my counselors."

When his soul clings to the dust please give him life according to Your word! When he tells You of his ways, answer him; teach him Your statutes! Make him understand the way of Your precepts and meditate on Your wondrous works.

When his soul melts away for sorrow—for he *will* be well-acquainted with grief if he is Yours—strengthen him according to Your word! He is ever surrounded by false ways in this age; teach him Your law! He has chosen the way of faithfulness; may he set Your rules ever before him. When he clings to Your testimonies, O LORD, let him not be put to shame! Enlarge his heart so that he may run in the way of Your commandments! (Psalm 119).

lmighty God, Please teach my husband the way of Your statutes; may he keep it to the end, as his reward. Give him understanding that he may keep Your law and observe it with his whole heart. Lead him in the path of Your commandments, and cause him to delight in Your path!

Incline his heart to Your testimonies, and not to selfish gain! Turn his eyes from looking at worthless things; and give him life in Your ways. Confirm to him Your promise, that he may fear You—fear You with every fiber of his heart. Turn away the reproach that he dreads, for Your rules are good. Behold, may he long for Your precepts; in Your righteousness give him life!

Let Your steadfast love come to him, O LORD, Your salvation according to Your promise; then shall he have an answer for anyone who taunts him, for he trusts in Your word. Sovereign LORD, may he trust the Bible with all his might! And take not the word of truth utterly out of his mouth, for his hope is in Your rules. May he keep Your law continually, forever and ever, and may he walk in a wide place, for he has sought Your precepts.

Make him also speak of Your testimonies before kings and be not put to shame, for he finds his delight in Your commandments, which he loves. May he lift up his hands toward Your commandments, and meditate on Your statutes.

Amen, come Lord Jesus (Psalm 119).

athcr of Wisdom,
Let me never cease to pray for my husband, asking that he may be filled with the knowledge of Your will in all spiritual wisdom and understanding, so as to walk in a manner worthy of You, bearing fruit in every good work and increasing in the knowledge of You. May he be strengthened with all power, according to Your glorious might, for all endurance and patience with joy, giving thanks to You, who have qualified him to share in the inheritance of the saints in light.

Do you remember, my beloved, that He has delivered you from the domain of darkness and transferred you to the kingdom of His beloved Son, in whom you have redemption, the forgiveness of sin? Yes, praise Him with me for His marvelous grace!

O LORD God, make him continue in the faith, stable and steadfast, not shifting from the hope of the gospel that he heard, which has been proclaimed in all creation under heaven. Keep him! Keep him! Keep him in the love of Christ. Amen (Colossians 1).

Anyone who would have power in prayer must be merciless in dealing with his own sins. ~R.A. Torrey

iver of all, Remember Your word to Your servant, in which You have made me hope. May my husband's comfort in his affliction be this: that Your promise gives him life. The insolent might utterly deride him, but do not let him turn away from Your law. When he thinks of Your rules from of old, let him take comfort, O LORD. O that hot indignation might seize him because of the wicked, who forsake Your law. And I ask that Your statutes would be his songs in the house of his sojourning. Cause him to remember Your Name in the night, O LORD, and keep Your law. May this blessing fall to him: that he will keep Your precepts.

When he kneels to pray, let him say, "You are my portion; I promise to keep Your words." I entreat Your favor with all my heart; be gracious to him according to Your promise. When he thinks on his ways, let him turn his feet to Your testimonies; may he hasten and not delay to keep Your commandments. Though the cords of the wicked ensnare him, do not allow him to forget Your law. And this I plead with fervent hope—that at midnight he would rise to praise You, because of Your righteous rules. Make him the companion of all who fear You, of those who keep Your precepts. The earth, O LORD, is full of Your steadfast love; teach him Your statutes! (Psalm 119).

God,
Blessed is the man who fears You, who greatly delights in Your commandments! Please continue to mold my husband into such a man.

Make light dawn in the darkness for him; You are gracious, merciful, and righteous. Grant that he deal generously and lend, conducting his affairs with justice. Let him never be moved; remember him forever.

May he be not afraid of bad news, but make his heart firm, trusting in You. Give him a steady heart, so that from the rising of the sun to its setting he will praise Your glorious Name.

O beloved, trust in the LORD! He is your help and your shield. O dear husband, trust in the LORD! He is your help and your shield. You who fear the LORD, trust in Him! He is your help and your shield. May you be blessed by the LORD, who made heaven and earth! We will bless You, O God, from this time forth and forevermore. Praise the LORD! (Psalm 112, 113, 115).

We are not so foolish as to think we can learn a trade without the diligent use of helps. Shall we think that we may become spiritually skilful and wise in the understanding of this mystery without making any real effort to use the helps God has given us? The most important of them is fervent prayer. Pray with Paul that 'the eyes of your understanding may be enlightened to behold' the glory of God in Christ. Pray that the 'God of our Lord Jesus Christ, the Father of glory, may give to you the spirit of wisdom and revelation in the knowledge of him.' Fill your minds with spiritual thoughts of Christ. Lazy souls do not get the tiniest sight of this glory. The 'lion in the way' deters them from making the slightest effort. ~John Owen

33

Great Upholder and Proprietor of all things, Please deal with my husband according to Your word. Teach him good judgment and knowledge, for he believes Your commandments. Even though he has gone astray before his affliction, assist him now to keep Your word. You are good and do good; teach him Your statutes. Although the insolent may smear him with lies, help him keep Your precepts with his whole heart; their heart is unfeeling, but he delights in Your law.

It is good for him to be afflicted, that he might learn Your statutes. And if this be what sanctifies him further, please bring suffering to him again. May the law of Your mouth be better to him than thousands of gold and silver pieces. Your hands have made and fashioned him; give him understanding that he may learn Your commandments. Those who fear You shall see him and rejoice, because he has hoped in Your word. O that such a lofty thought might be true! I know, O LORD, that Your rules are righteous, and that in faithfulness You afflict him. Let Your steadfast love comfort him according to Your promise.

Let Your mercy go to him, that he may live; for Your law is his delight. Let the insolent be put to shame, because they have wronged him with falsehood; as for him, may he meditate on Your precepts. Let those who fear You turn to him, that they may know Your testimonies. May his heart be blameless in Your statutes, that he may not be put to shame! Amen (Psalm 119).

timeless Light of lights, Eternal Father, Make my husband's soul long for Your salvation; may he hope in Your word. Be the cause of his eyes longing for Your promise; of his asking, "When will You comfort me?" Let him seek the deepest of comfort in Your steadfast love and faithfulness. When he becomes like a wineskin in the smoke, let him not forget Your statutes. How long must Your servant endure? When will You judge those who persecute him? The insolent have dug pitfalls for him; they do not live according to Your law. All Your commandments are sure; they persecute him with falsehood; help him! When they have almost made an end of him on earth, let him not forsake Your precepts. In Your steadfast love give him life, that he may keep the testimonies of Your mouth.

Forever, O LORD, Your word is firmly fixed in the heavens. Your faithfulness endures to all generations; You have established the earth and it stands fast. By Your appointment they stand this day, for all things are Your servants. If Your law is not made to be my husband's delight, he will surely perish in his affliction. Oh, that he would never forget Your precepts, for by them You have given him life. He is Yours, save him, for he has sought Your precepts. When the wicked lie in wait to destroy him, may he consider Your testimonies. I have seen a limit to all perfection, but Your commandment is exceedingly broad. Give him life in Your ways. Amen. Come, Lord Jesus (Psalm 119).

It is very apparent from the word of God, that he is wont often to try the faith and patience of his people, when crying to him for some great and important mercy, by withholding the mercy sought, for a season; and not only so, but at first to cause an increase of dark appearances. And yet he, without fail, at last succeeds those who continue instant in prayer, with all perseverance, and will not let him go except he blesses.
~Jonathan Edwards

What a blessed thing is the marriage of two believers, of one hope, one discipline, servants of the same Master! . . . Together they offer up their prayers - together they lie in the dust, and keep their fasts, teaching each other, exhorting each other, bearing up each other. They are together in God's Church, together at God's feast, together in straits, persecutions, consolations; freely the sick are visited and the indigent supported; there are alms without trouble; sacrifices without scruple; daily unimpeded diligence. Christ sees it and rejoices.
~Tertullian

hangeless God,

May my husband never forget all Your benefits.

Help me to remind him relentlessly of the One who forgives all his iniquity, who heals all his diseases, who redeems his life from the pit, who crowns him with steadfast love and mercy, who satisfies him with good so that his youth is renewed like the eagle's.

Please work righteousness and justice for him when he is oppressed. Make known Your ways to him, Your acts to Your precious son.

O beloved, hear again of our marvelous God! The LORD is merciful and gracious, slow to anger and abounding in steadfast love. He will not always chide, nor will He keep His anger forever. He does not deal with you according to your sins, nor repay you according to your iniquities. For as high as the heavens are above the earth, so great is His steadfast love toward those who fear Him; as far as the east is from the west, so far does He remove your transgressions from you.

O LORD, as a father shows compassion to his children, please show compassion to him. For You know his frame; You remember that he is dust.

Come quickly, Lord Jesus! Amen, we long and wait for You (Psalm 103).

There is nothing in which we need to take so many lessons as in prayer. There is nothing of which we are so utterly ignorant when we first begin; there is nothing in which we are so helpless. ~Alexander Whyte

overeign Creator and Sustainer, Oh how I love Your law! May it be my husband's meditation all the day. Your commandment makes him wiser than his enemies, for it is ever with him. Grant him more understanding than all his teachers by making Your testimonies his meditation. May he understand more than the aged, because he keeps Your precepts. Assist him to hold back his feet from every evil way, in order to keep Your word. May he not turn aside from Your rules, for You have taught him. Please cause him to say, "How sweet are Your words to my taste, sweeter than honey to my mouth!" Through Your precepts make him get understanding, and so hate every false way.

Your word is a lamp to his feet and a light to his path. May he swear an oath and confirm it, to keep Your righteous rules. When he is severely afflicted please give him life, O LORD, according to Your word! Accept his free offerings of praise, O LORD, and teach him Your rules. Though he may hold his life in his hand continually, let him not forget Your law. When the wicked lay a snare for him, may he not stray from Your precepts. Make Your testimonies his heritage forever, and the joy of his heart. Incline his heart to perform Your statutes forever, to the end. Amen (Psalm 119).

Sweet Sustainer and Rock of Salvation, I do not ask that You take my dear husband out of the world, but that You keep him from the evil one. Sanctify him in the truth; Your word is truth. Father, I desire that he also, whom You have given to Christ, may be with Him where He is, to see His glory that You have given Him because You loved Him before the foundation of the world.

I give thanks to You always for my husband because of Your grace that has been given him in Christ Jesus, and I ask that in every way he may be enriched in You in all speech and all knowledge—even that the testimony about Christ might be confirmed in him—so that he will not be lacking in any spiritual gift, as he waits for the revealing of our Lord Jesus Christ, who will sustain him to the end, guiltless in the day of Christ.

O God, be the source of his life in Christ Jesus, whom You made his wisdom and his righteousness and sanctification and redemption. Therefore, let him boast solely in You. For the display of Your wonderful winsomeness, Amen (John 17 & I Corinthians 1).

Desire gives fervor to prayer. The soul cannot be listless when some great desire fixes and inflames it...Strong desires make strong prayers...The neglect of prayer is the fearful token of dead spiritual desires...There can be no true praying without desire. ~E. M. Bounds

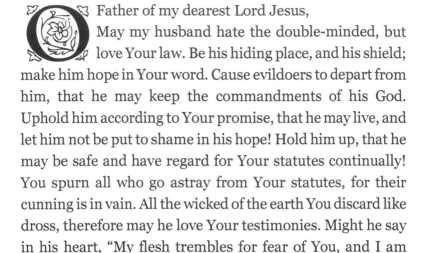 Father of my dearest Lord Jesus, May my husband hate the double-minded, but love Your law. Be his hiding place, and his shield; make him hope in Your word. Cause evildoers to depart from him, that he may keep the commandments of his God. Uphold him according to Your promise, that he may live, and let him not be put to shame in his hope! Hold him up, that he may be safe and have regard for Your statutes continually! You spurn all who go astray from Your statutes, for their cunning is in vain. All the wicked of the earth You discard like dross, therefore may he love Your testimonies. Might he say in his heart, "My flesh trembles for fear of You, and I am afraid of Your judgments."

He has done what is just and right; do not leave him to his oppressors. Give him a pledge of good; let not the insolent oppress him. May his eyes long for Your salvation and for the fulfillment of Your righteous promise. Deal with my husband, Your servant, according to Your steadfast love, and teach him Your statutes. He is Your servant; give him understanding, that he may know Your testimonies! It is time for You to act, for Your law has been broken. Therefore, may he cry in his heart, "I love Your commandments above gold, above fine gold. Therefore I consider all Your precepts to be right; I hate every false way." Amen, Come Lord Jesus (Psalm 119).

ur Father in heaven, Hallowed be Your Name. Please keep Your Name holy in the life of my husband. Cause him to consider it reverently in his mind and heart, treating it as sacred by his words and conduct.

May Your kingdom come, and may he long for the day of Your fullness far more than anything else in this life. Stir his heart to seek first Your kingdom.

Your will be done on earth as it is in heaven. Perform Your good pleasure in him—use him as a vessel to magnify the beauty of Your Son. Give him this day his daily bread, providing for his physical needs, for You are a loving, merciful Father who gives good gifts to His children. Teach him to trust You, being not anxious about whether he will have enough for tomorrow.

Forgive him his debts, as he also forgives his debtors. Forgive him when he falls short of Your glory. And form in him a pardoning heart, forbearing in everything.

Lead him not into temptation, but deliver him from evil. Rescue him from the deceitfulness of sin. By Your undeserved mercy keep his heart from being darkened and led into foolishness. For Yours is the kingdom, the power, and the glory forever! Amen (Matthew 6).

Giving God good advice, and abusing the devil isn't praying.
~L.M. Montgomery

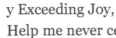 y Exceeding Joy,

Help me never cease to give thanks for my dear husband, remembering him in my prayers, that You, the God of my Lord Jesus Christ, the Father of glory, may give him a spirit of wisdom and of revelation in the knowledge of You, having the eyes of his heart enlightened, that he may know what is the hope to which You have called him, what are the riches of Your glorious inheritance in the saints, and what is the immeasurable greatness of Your power toward us who believe, according to the working of Your great might.

O LORD, he cannot know and delight in the mystery and beauty of Your gospel unless Your Spirit intervenes, bringing about fruit in him for righteousness. For this reason I bow my knees before You, Father, from whom every family in heaven and on earth is named, that according to the riches of Your glory You may strengthen him with power through Your Spirit in his inner being, so that Christ may dwell in his heart through faith—that he, being rooted and grounded in love, may have strength to comprehend with all the saints what is the breadth and length and height and depth, and to *know* the love of Christ that surpasses knowledge, that he may be filled with all of Your fullness.

Now to You who are able to do far more abundantly than all that we ask or think, according to the power at work within us, to You be glory in the church and in Christ Jesus throughout all generations, forever and ever Amen (Ephesians 1 & 3).

erciful LORD,
I know that it is Your good pleasure to give of Yourself to those who ask; therefore I pray that my husband's delight would be in Your law. May he meditate on it day and night. Teach him what it is to serve You with fear and rejoice with trembling.

O LORD, be a shield about him, his glory, and the lifter of his head. Assist him to put his trust in You so that his heart exults, saying, "You have put more joy in my heart than they have when their grain and wine abound." In peace make him both lie down and sleep; for You alone, O LORD, make him dwell in safety. Lead him, O LORD, in Your righteousness because of his enemies; make Your way straight before him. Let him take refuge in You and rejoice; let him ever sing for joy, and spread Your protection over him, that he who loves Your Name may exult in You.

For You bless the righteous, O LORD; You cover him with favor as with a shield. May he give to You the thanks due to Your righteousness, and sing praise to Your Name, Most High.

O beloved, give thanks to the LORD with your whole heart; recount all of His wonderful deeds! Be glad and exult in God; sing praise to His Name, the Most High.

For those who know Your Name, O LORD, put their trust in You, for You have not forsaken those who seek You. Remind him that he is but a man, wholly dependent upon You for life and breath and everything else. I commit him to You. Amen (Psalm 2, 4, 5, 9).

Thou Great I Am,
You are righteous; You love righteous deeds; the upright shall behold Your face. Therefore cause my husband to walk uprightly so that he might do what he was made for—behold Your wonderful face! May he trust in Your steadfast love; may his heart rejoice in Your salvation. And then let him sing to You, because You have dealt bountifully with him. Again I ask that he be constrained to walk blamelessly and do what is right and speak the truth in his heart.

O that he would say and continue to say to You, "You are my Lord; I have no good apart from You. You are my chosen portion and my cup; You hold my lot." May he set You always before him; trusting that because You are at his right hand, he shall not be shaken. Please make known to him the path of life; that in Your presence there is fullness of joy; at Your right hand are pleasures evermore.

Wondrously show Your steadfast love to him, O Savior of those who seek refuge from their adversaries at Your right hand. Keep him as the apple of Your eye; hide him in the shadow of Your wings. As for him, may he behold Your face in righteousness; when he awakes, may he be satisfied with Your likeness. Praise the LORD! (Psalm 11, 13, 16, 17).

No prayer is more powerful than the prayer of powerlessness, of littleness, of not knowing. Isn't this what it means to be poor in spirit? ~Mike Mason

triune God, I love You, O LORD, my strength. May You be to my husband his rock and his fortress and his deliverer, his God, his rock, in whom he takes refuge, his shield, and the horn of his salvation, his stronghold. You alone are worthy to be praised.

By Your mercy bring him out into a broad place; rescue him, because You delight in him. Put all Your rules before him, and may he never put Your statutes away from him. For it is You who light his lamp; O LORD my God, lighten his darkness. Make him abide in this precious promise: "This God—His way is perfect; the word of the LORD proves true; He is a shield for all those who take refuge in Him."

Give him the shield of Your salvation, and with Your right hand support him, and with Your gentleness make him great. With Your perfect law, O LORD, revive his soul. With Your sure testimony make him wise. By Your right precepts cause his heart to rejoice. And may Your pure commandment enlighten his eyes.

Keep him, Your servant, also from presumptuous sins; let them not have dominion over him! Let the words of his mouth and the meditation of his heart be pleasing in Your sight, O LORD, my Rock and my Redeemer (Psalm 18 & 19).

 nfinite Father,
It is my plea by the Name of Christ, that You hear me on behalf of my husband. Since he is one of Your holy and beloved chosen, then put on him compassion, kindness, humility, meekness, and patience. And if one has a complaint against him, let him forgive as You have forgiven him. And above all these put on him love, which binds everything together in perfect harmony.

And let the peace of Christ rule in his heart, to which indeed he was called. And may he be thankful. Let the word of Christ dwell in him richly, as he teaches and admonishes others in all wisdom, singing psalms and hymns and spiritual songs, with thankfulness in his heart to You. And whatever he does, in word or deed, may everything be in the Name of the Lord Jesus, giving thanks to You, his Father, through Him.

O beloved, continue steadfastly in prayer, being watchful in it with thanksgiving. I commit you to our dearest and fairest Lord Jesus. He will sustain you. Amen (Colossians 3 & 4).

ll-sufficient King,

May You answer my dear husband in the day of trouble! May Your great Name, God of Jacob, protect him! Grant his heart's desire and fulfill all his plans! May he shout for joy over Your salvation, and in the name of his God set up his banners! May You fulfill all his petitions.

Some trust in chariots and some in horses, but let *him* trust in the name of the LORD his God. Make him glad with the joy of Your presence. Be exalted, O LORD, in Your strength! Let him sing and praise Your power.

When trouble is near and there is none to help, be not far from him. For You, O LORD, are his Shepherd; he shall not want. Please make him to lie down in green pastures. Lead him beside still waters. Restore his soul. And by grace, lead him in paths of righteousness for Your Name's sake.

Even when he walks through the valley of the shadow of death, let him fear no evil, for You are with him; with Your rod and Your staff comfort him. May goodness and mercy follow him all the days of his life, that he may dwell in Your house forever (Psalm 20 & 23).

For my part, if I cannot pray, I would rather know it, and groan over my soul's barrenness till the Lord shall again visit me with fruitfulness of devotion. ~Charles Spurgeon

Life-giving God,
O that the husband You have provided for me would have clean hands and a pure heart! Guard him so that he does not lift up his soul to what is false or swear deceitfully. Guide him so that he might receive blessings from You and righteousness from the God of his salvation. Cause him to seek You, to seek the face of the God of Jacob.

To You, O LORD, I lift up his soul. O my God, in You I trust; let him not be put to shame; let not his enemies exult over him. Make him to know Your ways, O LORD; teach him Your paths. Lead him in Your truth and teach him, for You are the God of his salvation; for You he waits all the day long.

According to Your steadfast love remember him, for the sake of Your goodness, O LORD! Lead him in humility and what is right; teach him Your way. Instruct him in the way You should choose.

Your friendship, O LORD, is for those who fear You, and You make known to them Your covenant. And so I ask importunately that You would fill him with the fear of You so that he might be Your friend.

Cause his eyes to be ever toward You. Turn to him and be gracious to him when he is lonely and afflicted. O guard his soul and deliver him! Let him not be put to shame, for he takes refuge in You. May integrity and uprightness preserve him, for he waits for You (Psalm 24 & 25).

ord of Heaven, Cause my husband to walk in integrity. May he trust in You without wavering. Prove him, O LORD, and try him; test his heart and his mind. Manifest Your steadfast love before his eyes that he may walk in Your faithfulness. Redeem him and be gracious to him.

You are his light and his salvation; whom shall he fear? You are the stronghold of his life; of whom shall he be afraid?

O LORD, I love how You have made him Your habitation and a place where Your glory dwells. I pray that he would earnestly say with the Psalmist, "One thing have I asked of the LORD, that will I seek after: that I may dwell in the house of the LORD all the days of my life, to gaze upon the beauty of the LORD and to inquire in his temple."

Let his heart also cry, "Your face, LORD, do I seek." Hide not Your face from him. Cast him not off; forsake him not, O God of my salvation!

O beloved, wait for the LORD; be strong, and let your heart take courage; wait for the LORD! (Psalm 26 & 27).

Prayer often avails where everything else fails. ~R.A. Torrey

Sovereign Commander of the universe, You are my husband's only true strength and shield; in You may his heart trust and be helped; let his heart exult, and with his song give thanks to You. You are the strength of Your people; be the saving refuge of my husband. May You give strength to him!

When he is mourning, turn it into dancing; loose his sackcloth and clothe him with gladness, that his glory may sing Your praise and not be silent. O LORD my God, I will give thanks to You forever!

In You, O LORD, may he take refuge; let him never be put to shame; in Your righteousness deliver him! Cause him to rejoice and be glad in Your steadfast love. Make Your face shine on him; save him in Your steadfast love!

O my beloved earthly treasure, the LORD preserves the faithful; be strong and let your heart take courage, you who wait for the LORD!

Keep him, Father; I commit him wholly to Your Hand (Psalm 28, 30, 31).

Fountain of all good, Instruct my husband and teach him in the way he should go; counsel him with Your eye upon him. May Your steadfast love surround him because he trusts in You. Make him glad in You; make him rejoice as a righteous one, shouting for joy as one upright in heart!

Let all the earth fear the LORD; let all the inhabitants of the world stand in awe of You! For You spoke, and he came to be; You commanded, and he stands firm. Behold, how good it is that Your eye is on those who fear You, on those who hope in Your steadfast love. O that his soul would wait for You; be his help and his shield. Together, may our hearts be glad in You, because we trust in Your holy Name. Let Your steadfast love, O LORD, be upon us, even as we hope in You.

Cause him to bless You at all times; may Your praise continually be in his mouth. Let him say, "My soul makes its boast in the LORD; let the humble hear and be glad."

O beloved, magnify the LORD with me, and let us exalt His Name together! (Psalm 32, 33, 34).

How easily we convince ourselves that we are praying to the Lord when in reality we are locked in our own thoughts. We need to ask: If I'm happy, am I really rejoicing in Him, or am I rejoicing in my own self-satisfaction? If I'm worried or afraid, am I truly and humbly asking Him for help, or is my mind busy trying to work out some plan (however spiritual it may seem) for getting myself out of trouble. ~Mike Mason

earcher of hearts,

I ask with reverent joy and trembling that my husband—my incomparable divine gift—would taste and see that You are good! Blessed is the man who takes refuge in You! Be near to him when he is brokenhearted, saving him when he is crushed in spirit.

Say to his soul, "I am your salvation!" Then may his soul rejoice in You, exulting in Your salvation. May all his bones say, "O LORD, who is like You, delivering the poor from him who is too strong for him, the poor and needy from him who robs him?"

You have seen, O LORD; be not silent! O Lord, be not far from him! Then his tongue shall tell of Your righteousness and of Your praise all the day long.

Make him feast on the abundance of Your house, and give him drink from the river of Your delights. For with You is the fountain of life; in Your light do we see light. O continue Your steadfast love toward him, and Your righteousness to the upright of heart! Let not the foot of arrogance come upon him, nor the hand of the wicked drive him away.

Please fill him with grace daily, that his life might be a fountain of sweet water. Amen (Psalm 34, 35, 36).

God who hears the prayers of Your children, Only You can bring my husband to trust in You and do good, to dwell in the land and befriend faithfulness. Only Your Hand can turn his heart like a stream of water to delight himself in You so that You will give him the desires of his heart.

O beloved, listen to my entreaty: commit your way to the LORD; trust in Him, and He will act. He will bring forth your righteousness as the light, and your justice as the noonday.

Father, let him be still before You and wait patiently for You; not fretting himself over the one who prospers in his way, over the man who carries out evil devices. For his steps are established by You, when You delight in his way; though he fall, he will not be cast headlong, for You uphold his hand.

It is my humble plea that his soul would take hope in Your words through David: "I have been young, and now am old, yet I have not seen the righteous forsaken or his children begging for bread."

May his mouth utter wisdom, and his tongue speak justice. May the law of his God be in his heart so that his steps do not slip (Psalm 37).

Necessity!—I hardly like to talk of that, let me rather speak of the deliciousness of prayer—the wondrous sweetness and divine felicity which come to the soul that lives in the atmosphere of prayer. John Fox said, "The time we spend with God in secret is the sweetest time, and the best improved. Therefore, if thou lovest thy life, be in love with prayer." The devout Mr. Hervey resolved on the bed of sickness—"If God shall spare my life, I will read less and pray more." John Cooke, of Maidenhead, wrote—"The business, the pleasure, the honour, and advantage of prayer press on my spirit with increasing force every day." A deceased pastor when drawing near his end, exclaimed, "I wish I had prayed more"; that wish many of us might utter.
~Charles Spurgeon

ORD of the cloud and fire,

The salvation of my husband is from You; You are his stronghold in the time of trouble. You help him and deliver him; please deliver him from the wicked and save him, because he takes refuge in You.

Do not forsake him, O LORD! O my God, be not far from him! Make haste to help him, O Lord, my salvation!

O LORD, make him know his end and what is the measure of his days; let him know how fleeting he is! Behold, You have made his days a few handbreadths, and his lifetime is as nothing before You. Surely all mankind stands as a mere breath!

Hear my prayer—may he wait patiently for You; incline to him and hear his cry. Draw him up from the pit of destruction, out of the miry bog, and set his feet upon a rock, making his steps secure. Put a new song in his mouth, a song of praise to his God. May many see him and fear, and put their trust in You.

Blessed is the man who makes the LORD his trust. As for You, O LORD, do not restrain Your mercy from him; may Your steadfast love and Your faithfulness ever preserve him!

O beloved, hope in God! Amen (Psalm 37, 39, 40).

God most high, most glorious, Be pleased to deliver him! O LORD, make haste to help him! Let those be put to shame and disappointed altogether who seek to snatch away his life.

But may he seek You and rejoice and be glad in You; may he love Your salvation and say continually, "Great is the LORD!" You are his help and his deliverer; do not delay, O my God!

As the deer pants for flowing streams, so may his soul pant for You. May his soul thirst for God, for the living God.

When his soul is cast down and in turmoil within him, let him hope in You and praise You—his salvation and his God. By day You command Your steadfast love, and at night may Your song be with him, a prayer to the God of his life.

Send out Your light and Your truth; let them lead him; let them bring him to Your dwelling! Then take him to Your altar; let him delight in You as his exceeding joy and praise You with the lyre, O God, my God.

Why are you cast down, O my beloved, and why is your soul in turmoil within you? Hope in God; for He is worthy of praise, your salvation and your God! (Psalm 40, 42, 43).

Only he who is himself secure and happy in the Lord can pray effectively for others. ~Mike Mason

lector of Saints,

May my dear husband boast continually in You, and give thanks to Your Name forever. Please redeem him for the sake of Your steadfast love! Be his refuge and strength, a very present help in trouble. Therefore we will not fear though the earth gives way, though the mountains be moved into the heart of the sea.

O God, be near him so that he will not be moved; help him when morning dawns. Make him to be still and know that You are God. And then let him clap his hands, shouting to You with loud songs of joy!

Know, my beloved, that the LORD, the Most High, is to be feared, a great king over all the earth. Sing praises to God, sing praises! Sing praises to our King, sing praises! For God is the King of all the earth; sing praises with a psalm!

Cause him to think on Your steadfast love, O God. Your praise reaches to the ends of the earth. Your right hand is filled with righteousness. Let him be glad! Let this son of Judah rejoice because of Your judgments!

Ransom his soul from the power of Sheol, and out of him shine forth.

O beloved, shine forth the shimmering beauty of our Lord Christ! Amen (Psalm 46, 47, 48, 49).

Living God, Incline my husband's heart to offer You a sacrifice of thanksgiving. Have mercy on him according to Your steadfast love; according to Your abundant mercy blot out his transgressions. Wash him thoroughly from his iniquity, and cleanse him from his sin! Make him know his transgressions and in humility have his sin ever before him.

Purge him with hyssop, and he shall be clean; wash him, and he shall be whiter than snow. Let him hear joy and gladness; let the bones that You have broken rejoice. Hide Your face from his sins, and blot out all his iniquities. Create in him a clean heart, O God, and renew a right spirit within him.

Cast him not away from Your presence. Restore unto him the joy of Your salvation, and uphold him with a willing spirit. Then his tongue will sing aloud of Your righteousness. O Lord, open his lips, so that his mouth will declare Your praise.

O beloved, the sacrifices of God are a broken spirit; a broken and contrite heart He will not despise (Psalm 50 & 51).

Why are we called "adulteresses" in praying for something to spend on our pleasures? Because God is our husband and the "world" is a prostitute luring us to give affections to her that belong only to God. This is how subtle the sin of worldliness can be. It can emerge not against prayer, but in prayer—and fasting. We begin to pray and fast—even intensely—not for God as our all-satisfying husband, but only for his gifts in the world so that we can make love with them. ~John Piper

oly LORD,

Make my husband trust in Your steadfast love forever and ever. May he thank You forever, because You are saving him. O that he would wait for Your Name, for it is good.

Save him by Your Name, and vindicate him by Your might. O God, hear my prayer; give ear to the words of my mouth. Hide not Yourself from my plea for mercy! Sustain him as he casts his burden upon You; when he is afraid let him trust in You.

In You, whose word we praise, in You we trust; we shall not be afraid. What can flesh do to us? This we know, that You are *for* us.

O beloved, do not be afraid, for what can man do to you? God is *for* you! You need not fear.

Deliver his soul from death, yes, his feet from falling, that he may walk before You in the light of life. Be merciful to him, O God, be merciful to him, for in You his soul takes refuge; in the shadow of Your wings let him take refuge, till the storms of destruction pass by.

Fulfill Your purpose for him and be exalted above the heavens. Let Your glory be over all the earth!

Dearest beloved, sing and make melody with me! We give thanks to You, O Lord, among the peoples; we will sing praises to You among the nations. For Your steadfast love is great to the heavens, Your faithfulness to the clouds (Psalm 52, 54, 56, 57).

Changeless God,
Deliver my husband from his enemies; protect him from those who rise up against him. Then he shall sing of Your strength; make him sing aloud of Your steadfast love in the morning. For You have been to him a fortress and a refuge in the day of his distress. O my Strength, we will sing praises to You, for You, O God, are our fortress, the God who shows us steadfast love.

Hear my cry, listen to his prayer; from the end of the earth may he call to You when his heart is faint. Lead him to the rock that is higher than he, for You are a refuge, a strong tower against the enemy. Let him dwell in Your tent forever! Let him take refuge under the shelter of Your wings! Appoint steadfast love and faithfulness to watch over him!

May he wait for You alone in silence; from You comes salvation. You alone must be his rock and his salvation, his fortress; let him not be greatly shaken. His hope must come from You.

Trust in Him at all times, my beloved; pour out your heart before Him; God is a refuge for us (Psalm 59, 61, 62).

y Father,
May my husband earnestly seek You; might his soul thirst for You; make his flesh faint for You, as in a dry and weary land where there is no water. Let him look upon You continually, beholding Your power and glory. May he know that Your steadfast love is better than life, so that his lips may praise You.

Form him into a man who will bless You as long as he lives, lifting up his hands in Your Name. Satisfy his soul as with fat and rich food. And I ask that he remember You even upon his bed, and meditate on You in the watches of the night, his mouth praising You with joyful lips. Please be his help, so that in the shadow of Your wings he will sing for joy.

O beloved, let your soul cling to God, for His right hand upholds you! (Psalm 63).

How, then, do you pray? Do you ask God for your daily bread? Do you thank God for your conversion? Do you pray for the conversion of others? If the answer is 'no', I can only say that I do not think you are yet born again. But if the answer is 'yes'— well, that proves that, whatever side you may have taken in debates on this question in the past, in your heart you believe in the sovereignty of God no less firmly than anyone else. On our feet we may have arguments about it, but on our knees we are all agreed. ~J.I. Packer

Lord and King,
Let my husband rejoice in You and take refuge in You! Let his upright heart exult! Praise is due to You, O God—You who hear prayers. Blessed is the one You choose and bring near, to dwell in Your courts! Please secure his place among such chosen.

Shout for joy to God, my beloved; sing the glory of His Name; give to Him glorious praise! Say to God, "How awesome are Your deeds! So great is Your power that Your enemies come cringing to You. All the earth worships You and sings praises to You; they sing praises to Your Name."

May he rejoice in You, who rule by Your might forever. Test him and try him as silver is tried. Please, please do not reject his prayer or remove Your steadfast love from him! Instead be gracious to him and bless him and make Your face shine upon him, that Your way may be known on earth, Your saving power among all the nations. May he be glad, exulting before You, jubilant with joy! (Psalm 64, 66, 68).

od of Grace,

Make my husband sure of this: that You who began a good work in him will bring it to completion at the day of Christ Jesus. For You alone are my witness, how I yearn for him with the affection of Christ Jesus. And when I do not, assist me to yearn for him as I ought. It is my prayer that his love may abound more and more, with knowledge and all discernment, so that he may approve what is excellent, and so be pure and blameless for the day of Christ, filled with the fruit of righteousness that comes through Jesus Christ, to the glory and praise of Your name.

With special grace I ask that You would enable him to count whatever gain he has as loss for the sake of Christ. Indeed, make him count everything as loss because of the surpassing worth of knowing Christ Jesus his Lord. May he suffer along with me the loss of all things and count them as rubbish, in order that he may gain Christ and be found in Him, not having a righteousness of his own that comes from the law, but that which comes through faith in Christ, the righteousness from You that depends on faith—that he may *know* Christ and the power of His resurrection, and may share in His sufferings, becoming like Him in His death (Philippians 1 & 3).

lmighty God, Be to my dear husband a rock of refuge, to which he may continually come. For You, O Lord, are his hope. May his mouth be filled with Your praise, and with Your glory all the day. O God, be not far from him; O my God, make haste to help him! May he hope continually and praise You yet more and more. Let his mouth tell of Your righteous acts, of Your deeds of salvation all the day, for their number is past knowledge.

So even to old age and gray hairs, O God, do not forsake him, until he proclaims Your might to another generation, Your power to all those to come (Psalm 71).

Among all the formative influences which go to make up a man honoured of God in the ministry, I know of none more mighty than his own familiarity with the mercy-seat. All that a college course can do for a student is coarse and external compared with the spiritual and delicate refinement obtained by communion with God. While the unformed minister is revolving upon the wheel of preparation, prayer is the tool of the great potter by which he moulds the vessel. All our libraries and studies are mere emptiness compared with our closets. We grow, we wax mighty, we prevail in private prayer.
~Charles Spurgeon

lessed be the LORD, the God of Israel, who alone does wondrous things. Blessed be Your glorious Name forever; may the whole earth be filled with Your glory!

I come before You with this petition: that my husband would be continually with You—may You hold his right hand. Guide him with Your counsel, for it is perfect, wise, and good.

Cause these miraculous, marvelous words to pour from his soul: "Whom have I in heaven but You? And there is nothing on earth that I desire besides You." I know that his heart and his flesh will fail, therefore be the strength of his heart and his portion forever.

As for my husband, it is good for him to be near You; let him make You his refuge, that he may tell of all Your works. Continue to mold him into a man who fears You, for who can stand before You once Your anger is roused?

O beloved, remember the deeds of the LORD; yes, remember His wonders of old. Ponder all His work, and meditate on His mighty deeds.

Your way, O God, is holy. What god is great like our God? You are the God who works wonders; You have made known Your might among the peoples. O please work wonders on his behalf, and with Your arm redeem him (Psalm 72, 73, 76, 77).

od of peace,
It is my request that my husband would set his hope in You and not forget Your works, but keep Your commandments. Let him not be like this stubborn and rebellious generation, a generation whose heart is not steadfast, whose spirit is not faithful to You. Make his heart steadfast toward You and faithful to Your covenant. Thank You for being compassionate, atoning for his iniquity, and not destroying him; You restrained Your anger from him and did not stir up all Your wrath.

Remember that he is but flesh, a wind that passes and comes not again. Restore him, O God of hosts; let Your face shine, that he may be saved!

O beloved, call to Him who alone is your salvation! With all your might seek His wonderful, matchless face! (Psalm 78 & 80).

God has designed not only that prayer come to be, but that prayer sometimes be a necessary means for accomplishing the ends he has ordained. In other words, God purposely designed how things would work so that some of what he accomplishes can only be accomplished as people pray. ~Bruce Ware

Blessed Father,

My husband needs to need You. O that his soul would long, yes, faint for Your courts; that his heart and flesh would sing for joy to You, the living God. Give him a thankful heart, ever singing Your praise! Bless him with a grateful soul, exalting Your Name forever.

O beloved, sing aloud to God your strength; shout for joy to the God of Jacob! Raise a song; sound the tambourine, the sweet lyre with the harp.

LORD God of hosts, hear my prayer; give ear, O God of Jacob! Bring him into Your presence, for a day in Your courts is better than a thousand elsewhere. May he rather be a doorkeeper in Your house than dwell in the tents of wickedness.

Be his sun and his shield; bestow on him favor and honor. Withhold no good thing from him, because he walks uprightly. O LORD of hosts, blessed is the one who trusts in You! (Psalm 84).

Thou Giving God,
Be gracious to my husband, for to You do I cry all the day. Gladden the soul of Your servant, for to You, O Lord, do I lift up his soul.

Teach him Your way that he may walk in Your truth; unite his heart to fear Your Name. Turn to him and be gracious to him; give him strength, and save him.

O beloved, sing with me of the steadfast love of the LORD forever; with your mouth make known His faithfulness to all generations!

Make him walk in the light of Your face, exulting in Your Name all the day, exalted in Your righteousness. Teach him to number his days that he may get a heart of wisdom. Satisfy him in the morning with Your steadfast love, that he may rejoice and be glad all his days. Make him glad for the days You have afflicted him, and for as many years as he has seen evil. Let Your work be shown to him, and Your glorious power to his children. Amen (Psalm 86 & 89).

lorious God,
Let Your favor be upon my husband. Establish the work of his hands.

Be his dwelling place, Most High, and be his refuge, so that no evil shall be allowed to befall him. Command Your angels concerning him to guard him in all his ways. Because You hold fast to him in love, please deliver him; protect him because he knows Your Name.

When he calls to You, answer him; be with him in trouble; rescue him and honor him. With long life satisfy him, and show him Your salvation. Satisfy him with Your beauty.

Hear, my beloved, while I admonish you! Listen to me: there shall be no strange god before you; you shall not bow down to a foreign god. Go to the LORD! Open your mouth wide, and He will fill it. He will feed you with the finest of wheat, and with honey from the rock He will satisfy you (Psalm 90, 91, 81).

Prayer is the process of crouching down and making ourselves small before God. This downsizing is not an option; it is the only way to enter the kingdom of heaven. To grow in the Spirit is to become little in relation to more and more areas of life—marriage, family, church, work—until eventually it is possible to be little and childlike even in the presence of Satan and all his demons. For it is God, not you or I, who is bigger than evil.
~Mike Mason

aithful Creator,

May grace and peace be multiplied to my husband in the knowledge of You and of Jesus our Lord. May he grow in the grace and knowledge of our Lord and Savior Jesus Christ. When he suffers according to Your will, let him entrust his soul to a faithful Creator while doing good.

Let him not love the world or the things in the world, and may he keep himself from idols.

O beloved, do not love what is passing away more than your God! Instead build yourself up in your most holy faith; pray in the Holy Spirit; keep yourself in the love of God, waiting for the mercy of our Lord Jesus Christ that leads to eternal life.

Now to Him who is able to keep you from stumbling and to present you blameless before the presence of His glory with great joy, to the only God, our Savior, through Jesus Christ our Lord, be glory, majesty, dominion, and authority, before all time and now and forever. Amen (II Peter 3, I John 2, Jude).

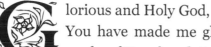

lorious and Holy God,
You have made me glad by Your work; at the works of Your hands I sing for joy. How great are Your works, O LORD, for You have made my husband! Your thoughts are very deep! Therefore keep him in Your care, and discipline him, and teach him out of Your law. For blessed is the man whom You discipline, to give him rest from days of trouble. Do not forsake him or abandon him as Your heritage.

If You are not his help, his soul would soon live in the land of silence. When his foot slips, hold him up, O LORD, with Your steadfast love. When the cares of his heart are many, cheer his soul with Your consolations. Become his stronghold, and his rock of refuge.

Oh come, my beloved, and let us sing to the LORD; let us make a joyful noise to the rock of our salvation! Let us come into His presence with thanksgiving; let us make a joyful noise to Him with songs of praise! For You, O LORD, are a great God, and a great King above all gods (Psalm 92, 94, 95).

If we do not learn to pray, it will not be for want of instructions and examples. Look at Abraham, taking it upon him to speak unto the Lord for Sodom. Look at Isaac, who goes out to meditate in the field at the eventide. Look at Jacob, as he wrestles until the breaking of the day at the Jabbok. Look at Hannah, as she speaks in her heart. Look at David, as he prevents now the dawning of the day, and now the watches of the night, in a hundred psalms. Look at our Lord. And then, look at Paul, as great in prayer as he is in preaching, or in writing Epistles. No, –if you never learn to pray, it will not be for want of the clearest instructions, and the most shining examples.
~Alexander Whyte

ord Christ,
Only by Your blood and imputed righteousness do I approach the Father with confidence concerning my husband.

Therefore, Father, as he received Christ Jesus the Lord, may he so walk in Him, rooted and built up in Him and established in the faith, just as he was taught, abounding in thanksgiving.

O beloved, if then you have been raised with Christ, seek the things that are above, where Christ is, seated at the right hand of God. Set your mind on things that are above, not on things that are on earth. For you have died, and your life is hidden with Christ in God.

Father, help him to walk in his new self, which is being renewed in knowledge after the image of its Creator. Assist him to put to death what is earthly in him: sexual immorality, impurity, passion, evil desire, and covetousness, which is idolatry. Let him put them all away: anger, wrath, malice, slander, and obscene talk from his mouth. You are the great healer and refiner. Purify my husband by whatever means are necessary. Make him wholly Yours. Amen (Colossians 2 & 3).

ORD God Almighty, Grant that my husband declare Your glory among the nations; Your marvelous works among all the peoples. For great are You LORD, and greatly to be praised; You are to be feared above all gods. Splendor and majesty are before You; strength and beauty are in Your sanctuary.

May my husband ascribe to You glory and strength! Let him ascribe to You the glory due Your Name, worshiping You in the splendor of holiness. Make him say among the nations, "The LORD reigns!"

Let him hear of Your righteousness and be glad, rejoicing with the sons of Judah because of Your judgments, O LORD. May he hate evil, for You preserve the lives of Your saints; You deliver them from the hand of the wicked.

O beloved come, let us worship and bow down; let us kneel before the LORD, our Maker! For He is our God, and we are the people of His pasture, and the sheep of His hand (Psalm 96 & 95).

Resolved, never to count that a prayer, nor to let that pass as a prayer, nor that as a petition of a prayer, which is so made, that I cannot hope that God will answer it; nor that as a confession, which I cannot hope God will accept.
~Jonathan Edwards

Eternal Father,
With Your right hand and Your holy arm please work salvation for my dearest husband. Remember Your steadfast love and faithfulness to Your son so that all the ends of the earth will see the salvation of his God.

Make a joyful noise to the LORD, my beloved; break forth into joyous song and sing praises! Join with the sea as it roars, with the world and those who dwell in it, with the rivers as they clap their hands, with the hills singing for joy together before the LORD.

O God, may he ponder the way that is blameless, and walk in integrity of heart. Let him not set before his eyes anything that is worthless, keeping a perverse heart far from him.

Do not hide Your face from him in the day of his distress! Incline Your ear to him; answer speedily when he calls! And by Your infinite mercy grant his heart to pour forth in song, "Bless the LORD, O my soul, and all that is within me, bless His holy Name" (Psalm 98, 102, 103).

It is crucial that we not be more fascinated, more gripped, by the prayers of a man than by the pleasures of God. How easy it is to be more thrilled by radical devotion than by divine beauty.
~John Piper

Bless the LORD, O my soul! O LORD my God, You are very great! You are clothed with splendor and majesty, covering Yourself with light as with a garment. And by the blood and mercy of Your perfect Son I appeal to Your wise power on behalf of my husband.

May his meditation be pleasing to You, for he rejoices in You. Let him thank You for Your steadfast love, for Your wondrous works to the children of men! Satisfy his longing soul; when his soul hungers fill it with good things. Send out Your word and heal him, and deliver him from destruction. Let him sing and make melody with all his being!

Awake, my beloved! Let us awake the dawn! Give thanks with me to the LORD among the peoples; we will sing praises to Him among the nations. For Your steadfast love, O God, is above the heavens; Your faithfulness reaches to the clouds. Be exalted, O God, above the heavens! Let Your glory be over my husband! Amen (Psalm 104, 107, 108).

LORD, Grant my husband help against the foe, for vain is the salvation of man! With You he shall do valiantly. O GOD my Lord, deal on his behalf for Your Name's sake; because Your steadfast love is good, deliver him! With his mouth let him give great thanks to You, praising You in the midst of sorrow. For You stand at the right hand of the needy, to save him from those who condemn his soul to death.

Praise be to You, LORD! I will give thanks to You with my whole heart, in the company of the upright, in the congregation. Great are Your works, studied by all who delight in them. Therefore help me to study my husband diligently, for he is Your wonderful handiwork.

Show him the power of Your works—that they are faithful and just; all Your precepts are trustworthy; they are established forever and ever, to be performed with faithfulness and uprightness.

O beloved, fear the LORD, for it is the beginning of wisdom; all those who practice this fear have a good understanding. His praise endures forever! (Psalm 108, 109, 111).

Divine Comforter,

When my dear husband sows in tears, let him reap with shouts of joy. Grant him assurance in the God of his salvation, hoping in You and Your steadfast love.

May he wait for You, and hope in Your word. Continually make him into a man whose soul waits for You more than watchmen for the morning.

O beloved, hope in the LORD! For with the LORD there is steadfast love, and with Him is plentiful redemption. Hope in the LORD from this time forth and forevermore.

Lord God, make me like a fruitful vine within our house, so that he will be blessed with children like olive shoots around our table. Your blessing be upon him! I bless him in the Name of the LORD!

I praise You, LORD, for You are good; I sing to Your Name for it is pleasant! For You have chosen my husband for Yourself; he is Your own possession. Do as You please with him; deal with him according to Your sovereign purpose. For I know that You are great, and that You are above all gods (Psalm 126, 130, 128, 135).

True religion makes us want to spend time alone in meditation and prayer. We read that this was true for Isaac (Gen. 24:63). Even more important, we read in the Gospels that Christ too needed to be alone with His Father. Concealing deep feeling is difficult, and yet grace-filled feeling is often more silent and private than that which is counterfeit. ~Jonathan Edwards

Living God,
Remember my husband even in his low estate, for Your steadfast love endures forever. Though he walks in the midst of trouble, preserve his life; stretch out Your hand against the wrath of his enemies and deliver him. Please fulfill Your purposes for him; Your steadfast love, O LORD, endures forever. Do not forsake the work of Your hands.

O LORD, search him and know him! Hem him in, behind and before, and lay Your hand upon him.

I praise You, for he is fearfully and wonderfully made. Wonderful are Your works; my soul knows it very well. His frame was not hidden from You, when he was being made in secret, intricately woven in the depths of the earth. Your eyes saw his unformed substance; in Your book were written, every one of them, the days that were formed for him, when as yet there were none of them.

Therefore take confidence, my beloved! The Almighty LORD of heaven and earth will accomplish for you what is best as His son. Faint not; be not downcast but sleep in His gracious providence, for when you awake He is still with you (Psalm 138 & 139).

I myself have seen this rare beauty on the face of a young woman at prayer, one who most likely had no idea that she was being seen by human eyes. Her countenance was incomparably more lovely than anything Hollywood's cosmetology is able to achieve. Indeed, divine grace working in a receptive soul does produce what St. Paul calls "God's work of art" (Eph 2:10).
~Thomas Dubay

Author of Salvation,

Being affectionately desirous of my husband, make me ready to share with him not only the gospel of God but also my own self, because he has become very dear to me. Now may You and the Lord Jesus direct his way, and make him increase and abound in love for all, so that You may establish his heart blameless in holiness before Yourself at the coming of our Lord Jesus with all His saints.

To this end I also pray for him: that You may make him worthy of Your calling and may fulfill every resolve for good and every work of faith by Your power, so that the Name of our Lord Jesus may be glorified in him, and he in Him, according to Your grace and the grace of the Lord Jesus Christ.

I ought always to give thanks to You for him, because You chose him to be saved, through sanctification by the Spirit and belief in the truth.

O beloved, to this He called you through our gospel, so that you may obtain the glory of our Lord Jesus Christ. So then, stand firm and hold to the traditions that you were taught by His word.

Now may the Lord Jesus Christ Himself, and You, Father, who loved him and gave him eternal comfort and good hope through grace, comfort his heart and establish it in every good work and word. Amen (I Thessalonians 3 & II Thessalonians 1 & 2).

od of hosts,
Restore my husband; let Your face shine, that he may be saved! Search him, O God, and know his heart! Try him and know his thoughts! And see if there be any grievous way in him, and lead him in the way everlasting!

Set a guard, O LORD, over his mouth; keep watch over the door of his lips! Do not let his heart incline to any evil, to busy himself with wicked deeds. Let a righteous word strike him—it is a kindness; let it rebuke him—it is oil for his head; let his head not refuse it.

May he cry out to You, O LORD and say, "You are my refuge, my portion in the land of the living." Attend to his cry, especially when he is brought very low.

Cause him to remember the days of old, meditate on all that You have done, and ponder the work of Your hands. Let him stretch out his hands to You when his soul thirsts for You like a parched land. Hide not Your face from him, lest he be like those who go down to the pit.

Let him hear in the morning of Your steadfast love, for in You he trusts. Make him know the way he should go, for to You I lift up his soul. Amen (Psalm 80, 141, 142, 143).

adiant Redeemer, Teach him to do Your will, for You are his God! Let Your good Spirit lead him on level ground! For Your Name's sake, O LORD, preserve his life! In Your righteousness bring his soul out of trouble.

I confess that he and I deserve none of these mercies, but only death and wrath. For what is man that You regard him, or the son of man that You think of him? Man is like a breath; his days are like a passing shadow. But praise be to You, Christ Jesus, for Your righteous obedience and perfect atonement.

O beloved, do you know His greatness? He is great and greatly to be praised, and His greatness is unsearchable. Extol Him as Your God and King. Every day bless Him and praise His name forever and ever.

Grant, Lord God, that he be a man who meditates on the glorious splendor of Your majesty and on Your wondrous works. A man who speaks of the might of Your awesome deeds, and declares Your greatness. A man who pours forth the fame of Your abundant goodness and sings aloud of Your righteousness. Amen (Psalm 143, 144, 145).

The magnificence of God is the source and measure of the magnificence of prayer. "Think magnificently of God."
~Alexander Whyte

ing of Kings, I appeal to Your testimony concerning Yourself: that You are gracious and merciful, slow to anger and abounding in steadfast love. You are good to all, and Your mercy is over all that You have made. Therefore, be eternally kind towards my dear husband. Keep him in the love of Christ, and let him give thanks to You and bless You always.

May he speak of the glory of Your kingdom and tell of Your power. Let him make known to the children of man Your mighty deeds, and the glorious splendor of Your kingdom. For Your kingdom is an everlasting kingdom, and Your dominion endures throughout all generations.

My beloved, *know* this God! He is righteous in all His ways and kind in all His works. Trust this God, for He is near to all who call on Him, to all who call on Him in truth. Love this God, for He fulfills the desire of those who fear Him, and preserves all who love Him.

Let his mouth speak Your praise, O LORD, and let all flesh bless Your holy Name forever and ever (Psalm 145).

In our Lord's prayer, he told us to pray, "Your kingdom come, your will be done, on earth as it is in heaven" (Matt. 6:10). This indicates that the perfect will of God precedes my praying and yours. We are not told to pray, "your will be formed," *but "your will be* done.*" ~Bruce Ware*

Prince of Peace,

Let my husband praise You as long as he lives; let him sing praises to his God while he has being. Let him be glad in his Maker, rejoicing in his King! Let him praise Your Name with dancing, making melody to You with his voice. Please take pleasure in his song and adorn him with salvation.

Let him exult in glory; let him sing for joy on his bed. Let Your high praises be in his throat and Your word in his hands. May he praise You in Your sanctuary; praise You in Your mighty heavens! Make him praise You for Your mighty deeds; praise You according to Your excellent greatness!

Put not your trust in princes, my beloved, in a son of man, in whom there is no salvation. But blessed is he whose help is the God of Jacob, whose hope is in the LORD his God, who made heaven and earth, the sea, and all that is in them, who keeps faith forever; who executes justice for the oppressed, who gives food to the hungry.

Everything that has breath praise the LORD! Praise the LORD! (Psalm 146, 149, 150).

Wise Counselor,

I ask that my husband would hear Your instruction and not forsake Your teaching, for they are a graceful garland for his head and pendants for his neck. All good things come from You, O God, therefore make his ear attentive to wisdom and incline his heart to understanding; yes, let him call out for insight and raise his voice for understanding, seeking it like silver and searching for it as for hidden treasures. Give him such fervor so that he might understand the fear of You and find the knowledge of God.

Let not steadfast love and faithfulness forsake him; bind them around his neck; write them on the tablet of his heart.

Trust in the LORD with all your heart, my beloved! And lean not on your own understanding. In all your ways acknowledge Him, and He will make straight your paths. Be not wise in your own eyes; fear the LORD, and turn away from evil.

Lord God, may he honor You with his wealth and with the firstfruits of all his produce; then his barns will be filled with plenty, and his vats will be bursting with wine. Let him not despise Your discipline or be weary of Your reproof, for You reprove him whom You love, as a father the son in whom he delights.

Finally, I am wholly dependent on You to keep him as mine alone. Empower him to serve me with all fidelity, drinking water from his own cistern, flowing water from his own well. For why should his springs be scattered abroad, streams of water in the streets?

Keep me also faithful to him. Cause his fountain to be blessed, and may he rejoice in me, the wife of his youth, as a lovely deer, a graceful doe. Let my breasts fill him at all times with delight, that he may be intoxicated always in my love. Amen (Proverbs 1, 2, 3, 5).

Better be somewhat too bold and somewhat unseemly than altogether to neglect and forget Almighty God. Better say that so bold saying, —"I will not let Thee go," than pray with such laziness and sleepiness and stupidity as we now pray.
~Alexander Whyte

Father of our Lord Jesus,
May You direct the heart of my husband to Your love and to the steadfastness of Christ. Work this miracle of grace in him: that he would count it all joy when he meets trials of various kinds.

If he lacks wisdom, let him ask You, who give generously to all without reproach, so that it will be given him. Cause him to be a doer of the word, and not a hearer only, deceiving himself.

Though he has not seen You, let him love You. Though he does not now see You, let him believe in You and rejoice with joy that is inexpressible and filled with glory, obtaining the outcome of his faith, the salvation of his soul.

O beloved, it is my greatest joy and privilege to remind you that you are of a chosen race, a royal priesthood, a holy nation, a people for God's own possession, that you may proclaim the excellencies of Him who called you out of darkness into His marvelous light. O remember! Once you were an orphan, but now you are God's child; once you had not received mercy, but now you have received mercy!

To You alone, Lord God, be glory forever! Amen (James 1 & I Peter 1 & 2).

od of Truth,

Please be my husband's confidence, and keep his foot from being caught. May he keep hold of instruction and not let it go; let him guard it, for it is his life. Make him commit his work to You so that his plans may be established.

O beloved, better is a little with the fear of the LORD than great treasure and trouble with it. The fear of the LORD is a fountain of life, that you may turn away from the snares of death.

Father, importunately I ask that he would find wisdom and get understanding, for the gain from it is better than gain from silver and its profit better than gold. May he consider wisdom as more precious than jewels, for long life is in her right hand; in her left hand are riches and honor. Let him not lose sight of these—sound wisdom and discretion, for they will be life for his soul and adornment for his neck (Proverbs 3, 16, 15).

There is no true prayer without agony. Perhaps this is the problem in many of our churches. What little prayer we have is shallow, timid, carefully censored, and full of oratorical flourishes and hot air. There is little agony in it, and therefore little honesty or humility. We seem to think that the Lord is like everyone else we know, and that He cannot handle real honesty. So we put on our Sunday best to visit Him, and when we return home and take off our fancy duds we are left alone with what is underneath: the dirty underwear of hypocrisy. ~Mike Mason

aker of Life,
For my husband's sake, and for the sake of Your great name, make me into an excellent wife. Because of Your sanctifying work may he consider me as far more precious than jewels. May his heart trust me, and may he have no lack of gain. Let me do him good, and not harm, all the days of my life. Empower me to work for him with willing hands. Give me vigor to rise while it is yet night and provide food for my household. Only by Your grace can I dress myself with strength and make my arms strong. Help me to open my hand to the poor and reach out my hands to the needy.

Let me open my mouth with wisdom, and put the teaching of kindness on my tongue. May I honor him by looking well to the ways of my household and not eating the bread of idleness.

May I be the kind of wife whose children rise up and call her blessed; the kind of wife of whom her husband says, "Many women have done excellently, but by grace you surpass them all!" (Proverbs 31).

ord and Father,

Thank You for calling my dear husband to belong to Jesus Christ. I praise You for loving him and calling him to be among the saints!

Grant that we may be mutually encouraged by each other's faith. And let him never be ashamed of the gospel, for it is the power of God for salvation to everyone who believes. For in it Your rightcousncss is revealed from faith for faith.

Indeed, when he was outside of Christ he failed to please You; he could not. He was not righteous, and there was no fear of You before his eyes.

O beloved, remember your depravity—the low estate from which He saved you! You have sinned and fallen short of His glory, and are justified by His grace as a gift, through the redemption that is in Christ Jesus, whom God put forward as a propitiation by His blood. And this was to show His righteousness, so that He might be just and the justifier of the one who has faith in Jesus.

Therefore he cannot boast, O LORD, for all that he has is of grace through Christ! May he live and breathe and eat and drink by grace alone, for Your glory alone (Romans 1 & 3).

God has made the spread of his fame hang on the preaching of his Word; and he has made the preaching of his Word hang on the prayers of the saints. This is the awesome place of prayer in the purposes of God for the world. The triumph of the Word will not come without prayer. ~John Piper

H oly Father,

Your servant David exults by saying, "Blessed are those whose lawless deeds are forgiven, and whose sins are covered." Therefore, please do not count the sin of my dear husband against him! I know that there will be tribulation and distress for every human being who does evil, and my husband has been wicked, as have I. We have had hard and impenitent hearts, thus storing up wrath for ourselves on the day of wrath when Your righteous judgment will be revealed. We have dishonored You by breaking Your wonderful law. Your name has been blasphemed among the Gentiles because of us. But thank You that for Your namesake You impute to my husband the righteousness of Your Son. By Your Holy Spirit keep him trusting in Christ's perfection alone, for You raised Him from the dead for our justification after He had been delivered up for our trespasses.

Therefore, my beloved, since you have been justified by faith, you have peace with God through our Lord Jesus Christ! O embrace and kiss Him! For through Him you have also obtained access by faith into this grace in which you stand. Let us, therefore, together rejoice in hope of the glory of God.

More than that, Father, help us to rejoice in our sufferings, knowing that suffering produces endurance, and endurance produces character, and character produces hope, and hope does not put us to shame, because Your love has been poured into our hearts through the Holy Spirit who has been given to us. Amen (Romans 2 & 5).

ncomparable God,

I praise You that while my husband was still weak and ungodly, Christ died for him. For one will scarcely die for a righteous person, but You have shown Your love for him in that while he was still a sinner, Christ died for him.

O beloved, since therefore you have been justified by His blood, much more shall you be saved by Him from the wrath of God. Rejoice! Rejoice in God through our Lord Jesus Christ, through whom you have now received reconciliation.

Father, let him not continue in sin so that grace may abound. May it never be! Do not allow him to live in sin once he has died to it. Cause him to consider himself dead to sin and alive to You in Christ Jesus. Let not sin reign in his mortal body, to make him obey its passions. Keep him from presenting his members to sin as instruments for unrighteousness. For sin will have no dominion over him, since he is not under law but under grace.

Just as he once presented his members as slaves to impurity and to lawlessness leading to more lawlessness, so now may he present his members as slaves to righteousness leading to sanctification. Instill this truth ever deeply within him: the wages of sin is death, but Your free gift is eternal life in Christ Jesus our Lord. Restrain him from earning deadly wages. And come quickly, Lord Jesus. We long for You. Amen (Romans 5 & 6).

Deliciously Gracious Master, When my husband finds himself divided in his desires, help him. There will be times when he delights in Your law in his inner being, but he sees in his members another law waging war against the law of his mind and making him captive to the law of sin that dwells in his members. And when he cries, "Wretched man that I am! Who will deliver me from this body of death?" make him hope in You through Jesus Christ his Lord!

O beloved, it is my joy to remind you that there is therefore now no condemnation for those who are in Christ Jesus. For the law of the Spirit of life has set you free in Christ Jesus from the law of sin and death.

O God, cause him to exult in the knowledge that You have done what the law, weakened by the flesh, could not do. By sending Your own Son in the likeness of sinful flesh and for sin, You condemned sin in the flesh, in order that the righteous requirement of the law might be fulfilled in us who walk not according to the flesh but according to the Spirit. Although his body is dead because of sin, give him life by the Spirit because of righteousness! Amen (Romans 7 & 8).

Pray often, for prayer is a shield to the soul,
a sacrifice to God, and a scourge for Satan. ~John Bunyan

Abba, Father,

I ask on behalf of my husband, that Your Spirit would bear witness with his spirit that he is Your child. For he did not receive a spirit of slavery to fall back into fear, but You granted him the Spirit of adoption as a son. Cause him to live according to Your Spirit and not according to the flesh. For if he lives according to the flesh he will die, but if by the Spirit he puts to death the deeds of the body he will live.

Please be faithful to bear witness with his spirit that he is Your child, and if a child, then an heir—Your heir and fellow heir with Christ, provided he suffer with Him in order that he may also be glorified with Him.

Therefore grant him the grace of strength to consider that the sufferings of this present time are not worth comparing with the glory that is to be revealed to him.

O beloved, be not discouraged when you groan inwardly as we wait eagerly for adoption as sons, the redemption of our bodies. For in this hope we were saved. Wait for it with patience.

O LORD, we long for the return of Your beautiful Son. Come quickly, Christ Jesus. Amen (Romans 8).

Beloved God,

By Your Spirit, help my husband in his weakness. For he does not know what to pray for as he ought, therefore may Your Spirit be faithful to intercede for him with groanings too deep for words. For You, who search hearts, know what is the mind of the Spirit, because the Spirit intercedes for the saints according to Your will.

O beloved, know for certain that for those who love God all things work together for good, for those who are called according to His purpose. For those whom He foreknew He also predestined to be conformed to the image of His Son, in order that He might be the firstborn among many brothers.

Father, thank You for Your sovereign choice; for loving him into faith in Christ, for predestining him to be conformed to His blessed image! Be magnified and lifted high for Your perfect work in him. Amen (Romans 8).

There is a general kind of praying which fails for lack of precision. It is as if a regiment of soldiers should all fire off their guns anywhere. Possibly somebody would be killed, but the majority of the enemy would be missed. ~Charles Spurgeon

Almighty Infinite Father,

If You are for my beloved husband, who can be against him? You who did not spare Your own Son but gave Him up for us all, how will You not also with Him graciously give him all things? Who shall bring any charge against him as Your elect? It is You who justify. Who is to condemn? Assure him with the truth that Christ Jesus is the one who died—more than that, who was raised—who is at Your right hand, who indeed is interceding for him. I praise You that no one shall separate him from the love of Christ. Even tribulation, or distress, or persecution, or famine, or nakedness, or danger, or sword shall not prevail over His love.

Do you trust His grasp, my beloved? Do you hope in the triumph of God alone, even when you are killed all the day long and regarded as a sheep to be slaughtered? For in all these things we are more than conquerors through Him who loved us. You can be sure that neither death nor life, nor angels nor rulers, nor things present nor things to come, nor powers, nor height nor depth, nor anything else in all creation, will be able to separate us from the love of God in Christ Jesus our Lord (Romans 8).

I have been driven many times to my knees by the overwhelming conviction that I had absolutely no other place to go.
~ Abraham Lincoln

ffectual Lover,

Your purpose of election must stand, for it is beautiful and wise to choose a people not because of works but because of Your call. May my dear husband learn to rejoice and tremble at Your words, "Jacob I loved, but Esau I hated." Let him not charge You with injustice because You are free. For You say to Moses, "I will have mercy on whom I have mercy, and I will have compassion on whom I have compassion." So then make him exult that it depends not on human will or exertion, but on You, who have mercy.

Let him love and fear the truth that You have mercy on whomever You will, and You harden whomever You will. Keep him from being a man who questions You with arrogance, or sets his ways of justice above You, or demands You to account for what he finds inequitable. May he not question his molder, saying, "Why have You made me like this?" For You are the Lord and potter, and to You belongs the right to make one vessel for honored use and another for dishonorable use.

O beloved, come, let us adore His goodness! In order to make known to us the riches of His glory He endured with much patience vessels of wrath prepared for destruction, to show His wrath and to make known His power.

Father, may Your Son be his greatest good forever. Amen (Romans 9).

reat Shepherd of Your sheep,

My heart's desire and prayer is that my husband may be saved. Let him never be a man who has a zeal for God, but not according to knowledge. Keep him from being ignorant of the righteousness that comes from You, and seeking to establish his own, thus failing to submit to Your righteousness. For Your Son is the end of the law for righteousness to everyone who believes.

Let this assurance ring afresh in his heart: that if he confesses with his mouth that Jesus is Lord and believes in his heart that You raised Him from the dead, he will be saved.

O beloved, adore the free goodness of our Lord's salvation! For the Scripture says, "Everyone who believes in Him will not be put to shame." For there is no distinction between Jew and Greek; the same Lord is Lord of all, bestowing His riches on all who call on Him. For "everyone who calls on the name of the Lord will be saved."

Father, You have told us that faith comes through hearing, and hearing through the word of Christ. Therefore use my husband to proclaim the good news so that his feet might be called beautiful. Amen (Romans 10).

Wise Husbandman,

Thank You for choosing my husband by grace. And if it is by grace, it is no longer on the basis of works; otherwise grace would no longer be grace. Thank You for sparing him from hardening, from a spirit of stupor, from eyes that cannot see and ears that cannot hear.

Make him humbly grateful that some of the natural branches were broken off, and he, although a wild olive shoot, was grafted in among the others and now shares in the nourishing root of the olive tree. Let him never be arrogant toward the branches, remembering that it is not he who supports the root, but the root that supports him. Do not allow him to become proud, but cause him to stand in awe. For if You did not spare the natural branches, neither will You spare him.

My beloved, note then the kindness and the severity of God: severity toward those who have fallen, but God's kindness to you, provided you continue in His kindness. Otherwise you too will be cut off.

LORD God, lest we be wise in our own conceits, help us to understand this mystery: a partial hardening has come upon Israel, until the fullness of the Gentiles has come in. May we tremble before Your sovereign hand that has consigned all to disobedience, that You may have mercy on all.

Oh, the depth of Your riches and wisdom and knowledge! How unsearchable are Your judgments and how inscrutable Your ways! For who has known Your mind, or who has been Your counselor? Or who has given a gift to You that he might be repaid? For from You and through You and to You are all things. To You be glory forever. Amen (Romans 11).

agnificent God,
I appeal to You by Your mercies, to receive my husband's body as a living sacrifice, holy and acceptable to You. And grant him the willingness to present his body in this way, as his spiritual worship. Let him not be conformed to this world, but transform him by the renewal of his mind, that by testing he may discern what is Your will, what is good and acceptable and perfect.

May he not think of himself more highly than he ought to think, but rather think with sober judgment, according to the measure of faith that You have assigned. Enable him to use his gifts according to the grace given him: if prophecy, in proportion to his faith; if service, in his serving; if he teaches, in his teaching; if he exhorts, in his exhortation; if he contributes, in generosity; if he leads, with zeal; if he does acts of mercy, with cheerfulness.

O beloved, let your love be genuine. Abhor what is evil; hold fast to what is good. Love with brotherly affection. Let us outdo one another in showing honor. Do not be slothful in zeal, be fervent in spirit, serve the Lord.

Lord God, only by Your sovereign grace will he be able to rejoice in hope, be patient in tribulation, and be constant in prayer. Assist us together as we strive to contribute to the needs of the saints and seek to show hospitality. Amen (Romans 12).

When thou prayest, rather let thy heart be without words,
than thy words without a heart. ~John Bunyan

wesome LORD,

Only by Your unmerited favor will my husband grow in likeness to Christ Jesus. So I entreat Your mercy on his behalf to enable him to bless those who persecute him; to bless and not curse them. Let him rejoice with those who rejoice, weep with those who weep, and live in harmony with his heavenly family. May he not be haughty, but associate with the lowly, giving himself to humble tasks. Let him never be conceited, nor repay anyone evil for evil. Instead grant that he give thought to do what is honorable in the sight of all. If possible, so far as it depends on him, make him live peaceably with all.

O beloved husband, never avenge yourself, but leave it to the wrath of God, for it is written, "Vengeance is mine, I will repay, says the LORD." To the contrary, if your enemy is hungry, feed him; if he is thirsty, give him something to drink; for by so doing you will heap burning coals on his head.

Holy God, do not let him be overcome by evil, but assist him to overcome evil with good; to cast off the works of darkness and put on the armor of light. Let him walk properly as in the daytime, not in orgies and drunkenness, not in sexual immorality and sensuality, not in quarreling and jealousy. But cause him to put on the Lord Jesus Christ, and make no provision for the flesh, to gratify its desires.

Come, Lord Jesus. We yearn for the day of Your unveiled beauty. Amen (Romans 12 & 13).

Thou who art faithful when we are faithless, Let my dear husband not live to himself. If he lives, may he live to You, and if he dies, may he die to You. So that whether he lives or whether he dies, he might be Yours. For to this end Christ died and lived again, that He might be Lord both of the dead and of the living.

O beloved, do not pass judgment on your brother, or despise your brother. For we will all stand before the judgment seat of God; for it is written, "As I live, says the Lord, every knee shall bow to me, and every tongue shall confess to God." So then we will both give an account of ourselves to God.

Therefore Father, let him not pass judgment on his brothers and sisters any longer, but rather decide never to put a stumbling block or hindrance in their way. Cause him to pursue what makes for peace and for mutual upbuilding.

Remind him of his obligation as a man of strength to bear with the failings of the weak, and not to please himself.

I ask, for the sake of Your Name, that through endurance and through the encouragement of the Scriptures he might have hope. May You enable us to live in such harmony with others, in accord with Christ Jesus, that together we may with one voice glorify You, the God and Father of our Lord Jesus Christ (Romans 14 & 15).

od of Hope,
May You fill my husband with all joy and peace in believing, so that by the power of the Holy Spirit he may abound in hope. Fill him also with goodness and with all knowledge, enabling him to instruct others.

I appeal to you, my beloved, by our Lord Jesus Christ and by the love of the Spirit, to strive with me in your prayers to God on my behalf, that I may be delivered from my propensity to wander from the narrow road, so that by God's will I may serve you with joy and be refreshed in your company.

I appeal to You, Lord God, to give my husband discernment and vigilance to watch out for those who cause divisions and create obstacles contrary to the doctrine that he has been taught; may he avoid them. Safeguard him from their smooth talk and flattery by which they deceive the hearts of the naïve. For his obedience is known to all, so that I rejoice over him, but I want him to be wise as to what is good and innocent as to what is evil.

Now to You who are able to strengthen him according to the gospel and the preaching of Jesus Christ, according to Your command, to bring about the obedience of faith—to You, the only wise God, be glory forevermore through Jesus Christ! Amen (Romans 15 & 16).

Pray, and let God worry. ~Martin Luther

hrist Jesus,

I praise You that in these last days God has spoken to us by You, His Son, whom He appointed heir of all things, through whom also He created the world.

Father, may my husband take pleasure in beholding Your Son as the radiance of Your glory and the exact imprint of Your nature, as He upholds the universe by the word of His power. May he exalt Him as much superior to angels as the name He has inherited is more excellent than theirs.

O beloved, join with me in saying, "Your throne, Lord Christ, is forever and ever, the scepter of uprightness is the scepter of Your kingdom. You have loved righteousness and hated wickedness; therefore God, Your God, has anointed You with the oil of gladness beyond Your companions."

You, Lord, laid the foundation of the earth in the beginning, and the heavens are the work of Your hands; they will perish, but You remain; they will all wear out like a garment, like a robe You will roll them up, like a garment they will be changed. But You are the same, and Your years have no end.

Father, cause him to adore Your magnificent Son incessantly and abound in thanksgiving for every glimpse of His beauty.

We long to see Him face to face (Hebrews 1).

Gracious Father,

I bow through Christ in prayer for the husband You have granted me. I have deserved death, but You have given me protection. I have earned hell, but You have provided a faithful husband for me. And for this I offer praise to Your great Son.

May my husband, who shares in my heavenly calling, consider Jesus, the apostle and high priest of our confession, who was faithful to You who appointed Him, just as Moses also was faithful in all Your house. For Jesus has been counted worthy of more glory than Moses—as much more glory as the builder of a house has more honor than the house itself. Now Moses was faithful in all Your house as a servant to testify to the things that were to be spoken later, but Christ is faithful over Your house as a son.

O beloved, we are His house if indeed we hold fast our confidence and our boasting in our hope.

Therefore Father, today, if he hears Your voice, let him not harden his heart as in the rebellion. Take care of him, lest there be in him an evil, unbelieving heart, leading him to fall away from the living God.

Help us to exhort one another every day, as long as it is called "today," that neither of us may be hardened by the deceitfulness of sin. For we share in Christ, if indeed we hold our original confidence firm to the end. Enable us to endure steadfastly! Enable us so that we might gain Your glorious Son!

Amen, come quickly Lord Jesus (Hebrews 3).

od of the living word,

Only through Christ, the great high priest, who is better than angels and greater than Moses—only through Him do I intercede for my husband. So I pray that while the promise of entering Your rest still stands he would fear lest he should seem to have failed to reach it. May Your good news meet with faith in him as he hears it.

I praise You that there remains a Sabbath rest for Your people, for whoever has entered Your rest has also rested from his works as You did from Yours. As the Scriptures say, "And God rested on the seventh day from all His works."

Let my husband therefore strive to enter that rest, so that he may not fall by the same sort of disobedience that overtook all those who left Egypt led by Moses. For Your word is living and active, sharper than any two-edged sword, piercing to the division of soul and of spirit, of joints and of marrow, and discerning the thoughts and intentions of the heart. And no creature is hidden from Your sight, but all are naked and exposed to Your eyes. And to You we must give an account.

O beloved, since we have a great high priest who has passed through the heavens, Jesus, the Son of God, let us hold fast our confession. For we do not have a high priest who is unable to sympathize with our weaknesses, but one who in every respect has been tempted as we are, yet without sin. Let us then with confidence draw near to the throne of grace, that we may receive mercy and find grace in our time of need (Hebrews 4).

plendid Savior,
It is my joy to trust and exalt You as the perfect source of eternal salvation to all who obey You.

Father, through Your Son I ask that my husband would never become dull of hearing, but instead crave solid food, developing skill in the word of righteousness. For solid food is for the mature. Therefore, please train his powers of discernment by constant practice to distinguish good from evil.

My beloved, let us leave the elementary doctrine of Christ and go on to maturity, not laying again a foundation of repentance from dead works and of faith toward God. And this we will do if God permits.

Therefore, Father, please be willing! Please permit him to go on to maturity. Keep him, and may he never be one who is enlightened, tastes the heavenly gift, shares in the Holy Spirit, tastes of the goodness of Your word, and then falls away. May it never be! (Hebrews 5 & 6).

I must secure more time for private devotions. I have been living far too public for me. The shortening of devotions starves the soul, it grows lean and faint. I have been keeping too late hours. ~William Wilberforce

od of boundless mercy,

May my dear husband live as land that has drunk the rain that often falls on it, and produces a crop useful to those for whose sake it is cultivated, so that he might receive a blessing from You. But have mercy on him lest he bear thorns and thistles, for such land is worthless and near to being cursed, and its end is to be burned.

Assure him of better things—things that belong to salvation. For You are not so unjust as to overlook his work and the love that he has shown for Your sake in serving the saints, as he still does. And I desire Your work in him, causing him to show the same earnestness to have the full assurance of hope until the end, so that he may not be sluggish, but an imitator of those who through faith and patience inherit the promises.

Convince him by the unchangeable character of Your purpose that he is an heir of the promise made to Abraham, that he might have strong encouragement to hold fast to the hope set before him.

O beloved, flee for refuge to Christ! For God has sworn by Himself and we have this promise as a sure and steadfast anchor of the soul, a hope that enters into the inner place behind the curtain, where Jesus has gone as a forerunner on our behalf, having become a high priest forever after the order of Melchizedek.

Lord Jesus, we exalt You as our hope and high priest! Please do not tarry in Your return (Hebrews 6).

lofty Lover of broken men, I come to You on behalf of my husband through Jesus, the guarantor of a better covenant. Instill within him the wondrous assurance that Christ holds His priesthood permanently, because He continues forever. Consequently, He is able to save to the uttermost those who draw near to You through Him, since He always lives to make intercession for them. May he entrust himself wholly to Him, for it is fitting that he should have such a high priest, holy, innocent, unstained, separated from sinners, and exalted above the heavens.

May he exalt Him, for He has no need, like other high priests, to offer sacrifices daily, first for His own sins and then for those of the people, since He did this once for all when he offered up Himself. For the law appoints men in their weakness as high priests, but the word of the oath, which came later than the law, appoints a Son who has been made perfect forever. Let him cling to Him all the more!

O beloved, be assured that you have a better spouse than I in Christ! For I pray for you in weakness, mortality, and with a wicked heart, but He is holy and perfect, and always lives to make intercession for you.

Father, assist us to love the Son's appearing (Hebrews 7).

There is not in the world a kind of life more sweet and delightful than that of a continual conversation with God.
~Brother Lawrence

God, my wealth and my salvation, Sink deep within my husband the understanding that he has a perfect and powerful high priest, one who is seated at the right hand of the throne of the Majesty in heaven, a minister in the holy places in the true tent that You set up, not man. For Christ has obtained a ministry that is as much more excellent than the old as the covenant He mediates is better, since it is enacted on better promises. Cause him to trust Christ's sacrifice alone, who through the eternal Spirit offered Himself without blemish to You. By His blood purify his conscience from dead works to serve You.

Take heart, my beloved, for Christ, having been offered once to bear the sins of many, will appear a second time, not to deal with sin but to save those who are eagerly waiting for Him.

Father, grant him such eagerness, that he may look forward to the day when his glorified Savior returns. May he exult in His sacrifice, offered once for all time for sins, after which He sat down at Your right hand, waiting for that time until His enemies should be made a footstool for His feet. O let him praise and prize Him! For by a single offering He has perfected for all time those who are being sanctified (Hebrews 8, 9, 10).

Prayer is as much a tool of our sanctification, by God's grace, as it is a tool of ministering God's grace to others. ~Bruce Ware

earful Judge,
Since my husband now has confidence to enter the holy places by the blood of Jesus, by the new and living way that He opened for him through the curtain, that is, through His flesh, and since he has a great high priest over Your house, let him draw near to You with a true heart in full assurance of faith, with his heart sprinkled clean from an evil conscience and his body washed with pure water. May he hold fast the confession of his hope without wavering, for You who promised are faithful.

O beloved, let us consider how to stir one another to love and good works, not neglecting our time together, as is the habit of some, but encouraging one another, and all the more as we see the Day drawing near.

Father, keep him from going on sinning deliberately after receiving the knowledge of the truth, for if he does there no longer remains a sacrifice for sins, but a fearful expectation of judgment, and a fury of fire that will consume the adversaries. Please, please prevent him from spurning Your Son, or profaning the blood of the covenant by which he was sanctified, or outraging the Spirit of grace! For I know that vengeance is Yours; You will repay. "The Lord will judge His people." Sustain him! For it is a fearful thing to fall into the hands of the living God (Hebrews 10).

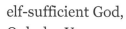 elf-sufficient God,

Only by Your worthy Son do I come to petition transforming and supporting grace for my husband. Make him grow in kindness and sympathy. Make him a man who has compassion on those in prison, and who joyfully accepts the plundering of his property, knowing that he has a better possession and an abiding one. Let him not throw away his confidence, which has a great reward. For he has need of endurance, so that when he has done Your will he may receive what is promised. I thank You that he is not of those who shrink back and are destroyed, but of those who have faith and preserve their souls.

Raise him up as a man of faith, having the assurance of things hoped for, the conviction of things not seen. For without faith it is impossible to please You, for whoever would draw near to You must believe that You exist and that You reward those who seek You. Make him like Abraham, who obeyed when he was called to go out to a place that he was to receive as an inheritance.

O beloved, even though men like Abel, Enoch, Noah, Abraham, Isaac, Jacob, Joseph, Moses, Gideon, Barak, Samson, Jephthah, David, Samuel, and the prophets were commended through their faith, they did not receive what was promised, since God had provided something better for us, that apart from us they should not be made perfect. And now we have the Lord Jesus Christ! Bless His name with me!

Father, we long to see Your matchless Son. Let us praise His name forever, to Your glory. Amen (Hebrews 10 & 11).

isciplining Father,

Assist my husband to lay aside every weight, and sin which clings so closely, and let him run with endurance the race that is set before him, looking to Jesus, the founder and perfecter of his faith, who for the joy that was set before Him endured the cross, despising the shame, and is seated at the right hand of Your throne.

O beloved, consider Him who endured from sinners such hostility against Himself, so that you may not grow weary or fainthearted. In our struggle against sin we have not yet resisted to the point of shedding our blood.

Great Father, remind him of the exhortation that addresses him as a son: "My son, do not regard lightly the discipline of the Lord, nor be weary when reproved by Him. For the Lord disciplines the one He loves, and chastises every son whom He receives."

Assure him that it is for discipline that he has to endure—that You are treating him as a son. For if he is left without discipline, in which all have participated, then he is an illegitimate child and not a son. May he not begrudge Your correction, but respect You and be subject to You, understanding that You discipline him for his good, that he may share in Your holiness. When Your discipline seems painful rather than pleasant, make him confident that later it yields the peaceful fruit of righteousness to those who have been trained by it (Hebrews 12).

entle and fearful Healer,

I bow through the merit of my Lord Christ, asking that You would lift my husband's drooping hands and strengthen his weak knees, and make straight paths for his feet, so that what is lame may not be put out of joint but rather be healed.

Cause him to strive for peace with everyone, and for the holiness without which no one will see You. May it never be that he fail to obtain Your grace! Protect him from any "root of bitterness" that springs up, causes trouble, and defiles many. Look after and guard his ways, that he may not be sexually immoral or unholy like Esau, who sold his birthright for a single meal. Have mercy! For I know that afterward, when he desired to inherit the blessing, he was rejected, for he found no chance to repent, though he sought it with tears.

O beloved, take refuge in Jesus, the mediator of a new covenant. See that you do not refuse the warnings of His Father. Flee to Christ, and you need not fear.

Father, help us as we strive to offer to You acceptable worship, with reverence and awe. For You are a consuming fire. Amen (Hebrews 12).

Satan trembles when he sees
The weakest saint upon his knees.
~William Cowper

aithful Helper,

Under the supreme sacrifice of Your Son I come on behalf of my husband. Please form him into a man who does not neglect to show hospitality to strangers, for thereby some have entertained angels unawares. May he remember those who are in prison, as though in prison with them, and those who are mistreated.

Let marriage be held in honor by us both, and keep our marriage bed undefiled, for You will judge the sexually immoral and adulterous. Maintain his life free from the love of money, and make him content with what he has, for You have said, "I will never leave you nor forsake you."

Therefore, my beloved, you can confidently say, "The Lord is my helper; I will not fear; what can man do to me?"

Father, remind him of his leaders, those who spoke to him Your word. May he consider the outcome of their way of life, and imitate their faith, for Jesus Christ is the same yesterday and today and forever. Guard him from being led away by diverse and strange teachings, for it is good for the heart to be strengthened by grace, not by the food of carnal wisdom, which has not benefited those devoted to it.

Hasten the day of Your Son's appearing, we pray. Amen (Hebrews 13).

My dazzling Delight,

Through Christ Jesus I ask that You would put a willingness in my husband's heart to bear the reproach Your Son endured. May he grow to love the world less and love You more; to love me less and love You more. For here we have no lasting city, but we seek the city that is to come. Through Christ then let him continually offer up a sacrifice of praise to You, that is, the fruit of lips that acknowledge His name. Let him not neglect to do good and to share what he has, for such sacrifices are pleasing to You.

Cause us to obey our leaders and submit to them, for they are keeping watch over our souls, as those who will have to give an account.

O my best beloved on earth, adore with me the God that gives you worth! He has made you ever precious in my eyes. May the God of peace who brought again from the dead our Lord Jesus, the great Shepherd of the sheep, by the blood of the eternal covenant, equip you with everything good that you may do His will, working in you that which is pleasing in His sight, through Jesus Christ, to whom be glory forever and ever. Amen (Hebrews 13).

My Sovereign Joy,

By Your beautiful Son and in His words I pray for my husband. May he be counted among the poor in spirit, for theirs is the kingdom of heaven. Make him of those who mourn, for they shall be comforted. Bless him with meekness so that he will inherit the earth. Create within him a hunger and thirst for righteousness, for such men shall be satisfied. Let him be merciful so that he may receive mercy. Give him a pure heart so that he might see You. Number him among the peacemakers, for they shall be called Your children. When he is persecuted for righteousness' sake, may he be heartened that he is blessed and that his is the kingdom of heaven.

O beloved, let me humbly remind you that you are blessed when others revile you and persecute you and utter all kinds of evil against you falsely on Christ's account. Rejoice and be glad, for your reward is great in heaven, for so they persecuted the prophets who were before you.

LORD, please be ever at work in him, molding him to be like Your Son. Amen (Matthew 5).

y gracious Father,
Through Jesus I kneel and ask that You would make my husband a brilliant light to the world. Let his light shine before others, so that they may see his good works and glorify You.

May he do Your commandments and teach them so that he will be called great in the kingdom of heaven. For unless his righteousness exceeds that of the scribes and Pharisees, he will never enter the kingdom of heaven. Keep him from becoming angry with his brother, from murdering him in his heart, and thus becoming liable to judgment. Keep him from looking at a woman with lustful intent, from committing adultery with her in his heart. If his right eye causes him to sin, let him tear it out and throw it away. For I would rather him lose one of his members than have his whole body thrown into hell. Instill within him a healthy fear of eternal fire.

Grant him humble longsuffering so as not to resist the person who is evil. If anyone slaps him on the right cheek, let him turn to him the other also. And if anyone would sue him and take his tunic, may he let him have his cloak as well. And if anyone forces him to go one mile, let him go with him two miles. Make him a man who gives to the one who begs from him, and who does not refuse the one who would borrow from him (Matthew 5).

oving Shepherd,

Please listen to my prayer because of Your Son's righteousness. I ask that You would incline the heart of my husband to obey His commands. May he love his enemies and pray for those who persecute him, so that he may be Your son. For You make Your sun rise on the evil and the good, and send rain on the just and on the unjust.

O beloved, if you love those who love you, what reward do you have? Does not even the world do the same? You therefore must be perfect, as your heavenly Father is perfect.

Lord, by Your Spirit continually work Your perfection in him! Help him to abstain from practicing his righteousness before other people in order to be seen by them, for then he will have no reward from You.

When he gives to the needy, do not let his left hand know what his right hand is doing, so that his giving may be in secret. For then You who see in secret will reward him.

And when he prays, keep him from being like the hypocrites who love to be seen and heard by others. Instead, cause him to go into his room and shut the door and pray to You who see in secret. Then, for what You see in secret please reward him. Amen (Matthew 5 & 6).

aithful Father,

Through Your Son I ask that You would keep my husband obeying His words. May he not lay up for himself treasures on earth, where moth and rust destroy and where thieves break in and steal, but make him lay up for himself treasures in heaven, where neither moth nor rust destroys and where thieves do not break in and steal. For where his treasure is, there his heart will be also. And I long for his heart to love You unswervingly as its Treasure. He cannot serve two masters; he cannot serve You and money. Therefore keep him always as Your joyful, loyal servant.

Let him not be anxious about his life, what he will eat or what he will drink, nor about his body, what he will put on. For life is more than food, and the body more than clothing. Turn his eyes to the birds of the air and remind him—they neither sow nor reap nor gather into barns, and yet You feed them. And he is of much more value than they! Remind him that he cannot add a single hour to his span of life by being anxious. Guard him from being anxious about clothing, for the lilies of the field neither toil nor spin, yet even Solomon in all his glory was not arrayed like one of them.

My beloved, trust your Master, lest He say, "O you of little faith." For if He clothes the grass of the field, which today is alive and tomorrow is thrown into the oven, will He not much more clothe you? Therefore do not be anxious, saying, "What shall we eat?" or "What shall we drink?" or "What shall we wear?" For everyone seeks after all these things, and your heavenly Father knows that you need them all. But seek first the kingdom of God and His righteousness, and all these things will be added to you.

Therefore, Father, may he not be anxious about tomorrow, for tomorrow will be anxious for itself. Sufficient for the day is its own trouble (Matthew 6).

I would exhort those who have entertained a hope of their being true converts—and who since their supposed conversion have left off the duty of secret prayer, and ordinarily allow themselves in the omission of it—to throw away their hope. If you have left off calling upon God, it is time for you to leave off hoping and flattering yourselves with an imagination that you are the children of God. Probably it will be a very difficult thing for you to do this. It is hard for a man to let go a hope of heaven, on which he hath once allowed himself to lay hold, and which he hath retained for a considerable time. True conversion is a rare thing; but that men should be brought off from a false hope of conversion—after they are once settled and established in it, and have continued in it for some time—is much more rare.
~Jonathan Edwards

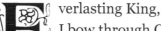 verlasting King,
I bow through Christ for the sake of the husband You have granted me. May he judge not, that he be not judged. For with the judgment he pronounces he will be judged, and with the measure he uses it will be measured to him. Guide him away from hypocrisy, to first take the log out of his own eye, so that then he will see clearly to take the speck out of his brother's eye.

Make him wise to avoid giving dogs what is holy, and to not throw his pearls before pigs, lest they trample them underfoot and turn to attack him.

Cause him to ask, so that it will be given to him; to seek, so that he will find; to knock, so that it will be opened to him. Thank You for Your promise that everyone who asks receives, and the one who seeks finds, and to the one who knocks it will be opened. Remind him that if he, who is evil, knows how to give good gifts to his children, how much more will his Father who is in heaven give good things to those who ask Him!

Whatever he wishes that others would do to him, help him do also to them, for this is the Law and the Prophets. May he enter by the narrow gate. For the gate is wide and the way is easy that leads to destruction, and those who enter by it are many. For the gate is narrow and the way is hard that leads to life, and those who find it are few. Keep him steadfast on the hard way! May he never stray from it! For Your namesake let his foot not slip. Amen (Matthew 7).

Righteous Father,
Please protect my husband from false prophets, who come in sheep's clothing but inwardly are ravenous wolves. Make him wise to recognize them by their fruits. Help him to discern the healthy tree by its good fruit, and the diseased tree by its bad fruit. May he not be a diseased tree, for every such tree is cut down and thrown into the fire. Therefore, help him to bear much good fruit.

Let the warning of Your Son safeguard and preserve him when He says, "Not everyone who says to me, 'Lord, Lord,' will enter the kingdom of heaven, but the one who does the will of my Father who is in heaven." May He not say to him, "I never knew you; depart from me, you worker of lawlessness." No! Instead, please let him hear the words, "Well done, good and faithful servant." Through Jesus and by Your wonderful Spirit I ask these things. Amen (Matthew 7 & 25).

The Spirit has much to do with acceptable prayer, and His work in prayer is too much neglected. He enlightens the mind to see its wants, softens the heart to feel them, quickens our desires after suitable supplies, gives clear views of God's power, wisdom, and grace to relieve us, and stirs up that confidence in His truth which excludes all wavering. Prayer is, therefore, a wonderful thing. In every acceptable prayer the whole Trinity is concerned. ~J. Angell James

Revealer of Truth,

Through Christ I ask that You would make my husband hear His words and do them, so that he may be like a wise man who built his house on a rock. Keep him from merely hearing His words and not doing them, for then he will be like the foolish man who built his house on the sand. When the rain falls, and the floods come, and the winds blow and beat against him, I do not wish him to fall! Your Word alone stands firm. May he build his life upon it.

Let him never despise or neglect tax collectors and sinners. But instead fill him with tenderness and compassion for them, and the humility to eat with them. For those who are well have no need of a physician, but those who are sick. Continue to teach him what this means: "I desire mercy, and not sacrifice." For Your great Son came not to call the righteous, but sinners (Matthew 7 & 9).

My Supreme and Everlasting Joy,
In this world my husband is as a sheep in the midst of wolves, so please help him to be wise as a serpent and innocent as a dove. Prepare him for the persecution that lies along his pathway to heaven. Strengthen him to stand fast when men deliver him over to courts and flog him in their churches.

O beloved, when you are dragged before governors and kings for Christ's sake, do not be anxious how you are to speak or what you are to say, for what you are to say will be given to you in that hour. For it is not you who speak, but the Spirit of your Father speaking through you.

Lord God, make ready his heart for that dreadful time when brother will deliver brother over to death, and the father his child, and children will rise up against parents and have them put to death, and he will be hated by all for the sake of Christ's name. May he endure to the end and so be saved! Keep him! For Your hand is mightier than my own. Amen (Matthew 10).

Prayer—secret, fervent, believing prayer—lies at the root of all personal godliness. ~William Carey

electable God,

Grant my dear husband the grace to love Christ more than his father or mother, more than his son or daughter. For Your Son has said that if he fails to love Him supremely, he is not worthy of Him. And if he does not take his cross and follow Him, he is not worthy of Him. Therefore, because of Your grace and steadfast love, enable him to do so!

May he not find his life in this world and so lose it, but make him a man who gladly loses his life for Jesus' sake so that he might find it.

Father, I know that it pleases You well to hide things from the wise and understanding and reveal them to little children. Therefore please grow him in childlikeness, show him Your matchless Son, and may He choose to reveal You increasingly to him.

O beloved, you who labor and are heavy laden, go to Christ, and He will give you rest. Take His yoke upon you, and learn from Him, for He is gentle and lowly in heart, and you will find rest for your soul.

Lord Christ, we praise and thank You that Your yoke is easy, and Your burden is light! (Matthew 10 & 11).

reat Covenant Keeper,

My husband cannot speak good if he is evil. For out of the abundance of the heart the mouth speaks. Therefore fill him with good treasure so that he might bring forth good. Make Christ his Treasure, so that he might speak His praise. For on the day of judgment he will give account for every careless word he speaks; so please do not let him be condemned by his words.

I praise You that to him it has been given to know the secrets of the kingdom of heaven, for to many it has not been given. Let him never be among those of whom it is said, "Seeing they do not see, and hearing they do not hear, nor do they understand." Keep his heart from growing dull. Help him to see with his eyes and hear with his ears and understand with his heart and turn, that You may heal him.

O beloved, your master Jesus has said that blessed are your eyes, for they see, and your ears, for they hear. Truly, I say to you, many prophets and righteous people longed to see what you see, and did not see it, and to hear what you hear, and did not hear it.

Father, it is You who have opened his eyes to behold the wonders of Your word and the glories of Your Son. Keep him vigilant. Amen (Matthew 12 & 13).

*No man can do me a truer kindness in this world
than to pray for me.* ~Charles Spurgeon

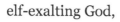

elf-exalting God,

May my husband never prove himself to be as one who, when he hears the word of the kingdom and does not understand it, the evil one comes and snatches away what has been sown in his heart. Guard him from the evil one! And let him not be like the one who hears the word and immediately receives it with joy, yet he has no root in himself, but endures for a while, and when tribulation or persecution arises on account of the word, immediately he falls away. Do not let him fall! Please grow his roots strong and deep in You.

Save him from being a man who hears the word, but the cares of the world and the deceitfulness of riches choke the word, and it proves unfruitful. Instead, make his heart good soil, so that he hears the word and understands it, and bears fruit and yields a hundredfold (Matthew 13).

overeign Ruler and King,
Your Kingdom is like treasure hidden in a field, which a man found and covered up. Therefore, may my husband be like that man, who, in his joy went and sold all that he had and bought the field.

Again, make him like the merchant in search of fine pearls, who, on finding one pearl of great value, went and sold all that he had and bought it. Let him count Christ his greatest treasure, his most valuable pearl, his ultimate source of joy. And may he stop at nothing to have Him.

Keep him from breaking Your commandments for the sake of tradition. May he never, for the sake of tradition, make void Your word. Indeed, unless You preserve him with grace he will be numbered among the hypocrites who honor You with their lips, but their heart is far from You; who worship You in vain, teaching as doctrines the commandments of men.

Let him take heart, and not be afraid, for it is You who keep him. Let him not doubt, for truly Jesus, the Son of God, is his righteousness (Matthew 13, 14, 15).

No praying man or woman accomplishes so much with so little expenditure of time as when he or she is praying.
~A.E. McAdam

Lord of the heavens and the earth, I come to You now petitioning more grace for my husband. His heart needs continual cleansing, as does mine, because what proceeds from it is what defiles a person. For out of the heart come evil thoughts, murder, adultery, sexual immorality, theft, false witness, slander. These are what defile a person, therefore please create in him a clean heart.

O beloved, guard your heart. Watch and beware of the leaven of the Pharisees and Sadducees, of the sophistry of this age, of the false teachers who speak sweetly and humbly. Blessed are you if you know the truth of Christ. For flesh and blood has not revealed Him to you, but your Father who is in heaven.

O God, may he set his mind on the things of You, and not on the things of man. All this I ask in the name of the Christ, the Son of the living God. Amen (Matthew 15 & 16).

y Mighty Fortress,
Thank You for giving me a husband who follows Your Son so faithfully. Assist him to continue going after Him, to deny himself and take up his cross and follow Him. May he not strive to save his life and so lose it, but let him lose his life for Jesus' sake so that he might find it.

O beloved, what will it profit you if you gain the whole world and forfeit your life? Or what shall you give in return for your life? For the Son of man is going to come with His angels in the glory of His Father, and then He will repay you according to what you have done.

Therefore, Father, cause him to continually consider Christ as more precious than life itself. For indeed He is! Remind him that unless he turns and becomes like a child, he will never enter the kingdom of heaven. Help him to constantly humble himself like a child, for such who do so are greatest in the kingdom of heaven. Amen (Matthew 16 & 18).

All hell is vanquished when the believer bows his knee in importunate supplication. Beloved brethren, let us pray. We cannot all argue, but we can all pray; we cannot all be leaders, but we can all be pleaders; we cannot all be mighty in rhetoric, but we can all be prevalent in prayer. I would sooner see you eloquent with God than with men. Prayer links us with the Eternal, the Omnipotent, the Infinite, and hence it is our chief resort. . . . Be sure that you are with God, and then you may be sure that God is with you. ~Charles Spurgeon

oly Lord,

Compared to the rest of the world my husband is astonishingly rich. And only with difficulty will a rich person enter the kingdom of heaven. Therefore, if he will be saved, You must do what is impossible with man—give him a heart that cherishes You more than money, possessions, or comfort. Help him! For it is easier for a camel to go through the eye of a needle than for a rich person to enter Your kingdom. Praise be to Your name that with You all things are possible—that he and I may be saved!

Grant him the grace to leave houses or brothers or sisters or father or mother or children or lands, for the sake of Christ's name, so that he might receive a hundredfold and inherit eternal life. Amen (Matthew 19).

Soul-Satisfying God,
I desire true greatness for my husband. May he seek to be a servant and slave, even as the Son of Man came not to be served but to serve, and to give His life as a ransom for many.

Please keep him loving You with all his heart and with all his soul and with all his mind. For that is the great and first commandment. And continue stirring him to love his neighbor as himself.

O Father, even as You grant him grace to adore You more, protect him from becoming a man who preaches, but does not practice. May he never tie up heavy burdens, hard to bear, and lay them on people's shoulders, and then be unwilling to move them with his finger. Instead, enable him to humbly offer himself as their servant. Amen (Matthew 20 & 23).

I have so much business I cannot get on without spending three hours daily in prayer. ~Martin Luther

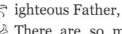ighteous Father,

There are so many pitfalls of hypocrisy that threaten to destroy my husband. You alone can guard his footsteps from straying from the narrow path. Let him never become one who does all his deeds to be seen by others, loving the place of honor at feasts and the admiration of churches and greetings in the marketplaces and being called wise by others.

O beloved, do not glory in your wisdom, for all you have is because of Jesus. For you have an instructor, the Christ. Whoever exalts himself will be humbled, and whoever humbles himself will be exalted.

Again, Father, may he never shut the kingdom of heaven in people's faces. Spare him from becoming a child of hell! Have mercy and save him from such woe (Matthew 23).

Thou who art beauty's fairest pleasure, Protect my husband. He dwells in a deceitful world; guard his mind. Keep him safe from blind guides and blind fools. Save him from following those who tithe generously and have neglected the weightier matters of the law: justice and mercy and faithfulness. May he not neglect these things, lest he be like the blind guides who strain out a gnat and swallow a camel!

Shield him also from the snare of merely external righteousness, like those who clean the outside of the cup and plate, but inside they are full of greed and self-indulgence. Please make him clean inside, that his outside also may be clean. Again, preserve him from becoming like a whitewashed tomb, which outwardly appears beautiful, but within is full of dead people's bones and all uncleanness. Woe to him if You do not rescue him from being one who outwardly appears righteous to others, but within is full of hypocrisy and lawlessness (Matthew 23).

Prayer is designed by God to display his fullness and our need.
Prayer glorifies God because it puts us in the position of the
thirsty and God in the position of the all-supplying fountain.
~John Piper

ighty Ruler,

Please, because of Christ, hear my prayer, and see that no one leads my husband astray. For many will come in Jesus' name, saying, "I am the Christ," and they will lead many astray. And when he hears of wars and rumors of wars, see that he is not alarmed.

O beloved, do not be surprised or afraid when kingdoms deliver us up to tribulation and put us to death. For the Son has warned us that we will be hated by all nations for His name's sake.

O Father, when many then fall away and betray one another and hate one another, let him not be one of them! Protect him from the many false prophets that will arise and lead many astray. And when lawlessness increases, do not let his love grow cold. But help him to endure to the end and be saved, and proclaim the gospel of the kingdom throughout the whole world as a testimony to all nations. Amen (Matthew 24).

insome Lord,
May my husband be like one of the wise virgins, who took flasks of oil with their lamps. So that when the cry comes at midnight, "Here is the bridegroom! Come out to meet Him," he may be ready to rise and go with Him to the marriage feast. Please keep him from being like the foolish virgins who took no oil, and so came late to the marriage feast. And finding the door shut, they were not allowed to enter.

O beloved, watch therefore, for you know neither the day nor the hour.

Again, Father, make him like the servants who doubled that with which their master had entrusted them before he went on a long journey. May he deal wisely with what You have given him, so that when You return You will say, "Well done, good and faithful servant. You have been faithful over a little; I will set you over much. Enter into the joy of your Master." Keep him from being like the worthless, wicked, slothful servant who was cast into the outer darkness where there will be weeping and gnashing of teeth. Please preserve him by grace and wisdom.

Come quickly, Bridegroom and Master! Amen (Matthew 25).

You cannot simply manipulate God by the power of being confident in what you ask. There are moral guidelines. This is what Jesus is saying with the condition, "If . . . my words abide in you, ask whatever you wish, and it will be done for you" (John 15:7). The words of Jesus shape the attitude and content of our prayers. ~John Piper

O Lover of the sheep,
Only You can keep my husband for Jesus Christ when He comes in His glory and sits on His glorious throne. So I ask that You would preserve him as one of Your sheep, to whom the Son of Man will say on that day, "Come, you who are blessed by My Father, inherit the kingdom prepared for you from the foundation of the world."

May he be a man who feeds the hungry, gives drink to the thirsty, welcomes the stranger, clothes the naked, and visits the sick and imprisoned.

O beloved, truly, I say to you, as you do it to one of the least of these, you do it to Christ.

Father, it is my fervent desire that he be such a righteous man so that he might enter into eternal life. Thank You for the promise that, as he strives to enter by the narrow gate, Christ is with him always, to the end of the age.

Our great Savior and King, we long for Your return. Amen (Matthew 25 & 28).

Lord and Husband,

When my husband strays from Your love, however wicked his waywardness proves to be, please draw him back! Even when he forgets You, allure him, and bring him into the wilderness, and speak tenderly to him. Make the Valley of Trouble a door of hope for him. May he answer You as in the days of his youth, as at the time when he came out of the land of bondage. And let him call You "My Husband." Make him lie down in safety and remind him that You have betrothed him to Yourself forever.

O beloved, forsake not your Husband! For He has betrothed you to Himself in righteousness and in justice, in steadfast love and in mercy. He has betrothed you to Himself in faithfulness. And you have known Him!

Father, be pleased to guard him from abandoning faithfulness, steadfast love, and the knowledge of You. Save him from being destroyed for lack of knowledge, from forsaking You to cherish whoredom, wine, and new wine, which take away the understanding. Preserve us both, for a people without understanding shall come to ruin (Hosea 2 & 4).

Praying is the same to the new creature as crying is to the natural. The child is not learned by art or example to cry, but instructed by nature; it comes into the world crying. Praying is not a lesson got by forms and rules of art, but flowing from principles of new life itself. ~William Gurnall

138

Redeeming Lover,

    I thank You that, even when my husband played the whore and did not know You, and even as he stumbled in his guilt, You knew him, and his way was not hidden from You. Graciously You tore him that You might heal him; You struck him down, and You bound his wounds. Then You revived him and raised him up, that he might live before You. Praise be to You, LORD God! For You made him acknowledge his guilt and seek Your face. You caused him to turn to Yourself and to seek You earnestly in his distress.

    O beloved, let us know; let us press on to know the LORD; His going out is sure as the dawn; He will come to us as the showers, as the spring rains that water the earth.

    And now LORD God, let him not resemble Ephraim and Judah, whose love was like the morning cloud, like the dew that goes early away. Increase within him steadfast love for Your name. For You desire steadfast love and not sacrifice, the knowledge of God rather than burnt offerings. Prevent him from defiling himself with other lovers. And continue to restore him. Amen (Hosea 5, 6, 7).

ost Holy Judge,
My husband is not immune to the subtle deceitfulness of sin. Therefore please protect him; increase his wisdom. Let him not be like a dove, silly and without sense. Woe to him if he strays from You! Only destruction will he find if You do not keep him.

May he never cry falsely, "My God, I—Your son—know You," when he has transgressed Your covenant and rebelled against Your law. Restrain him from making idols with his silver and gold. And forbid that he ever become incapable of innocence.

O beloved, cling to your righteous Husband! Fear the LORD and turn away from evil, lest you find yourself to be a useless vessel, and begin to regard His laws as a strange thing.

Father, may he not forget his Maker! Let him not grow to love a prostitute's wages. May he consecrate himself always to You and not to anything shameful, lest he become detestable like the thing he loves. Preserve his glory and righteousness. Accept him because he listens to You, and make him bear much fruit in Your house. Show Your love to him, that his children may see many days (Hosea 7, 8, 9).

Cold prayers always freeze before they reach heaven.
~Thomas Brooks

Merciful Leader of wayward children, Thank You for growing my husband into a luxuriant vine that yields its fruit. You have dealt bountifully in giving him to me. But as his fruit increases, may he not use it to improve his pursuit of self or foreign altars. Guard his heart from becoming false, saying, "I have no king, for I do not fear the LORD." Such is the danger if You do not keep him. Unless You continue with him he will utter mere words; with empty oaths he will make covenants. Let him not be put to shame!

O beloved, He has kindly spared your neck. Do not make Him put you to the yoke to plow and harrow for yourself. Instead, sow for yourself righteousness; reap steadfast love.

LORD God, break up his fallow ground and let him seek You, that You may come and rain righteousness upon him.

Have mercy on us, for we have together plowed iniquity; we have reaped injustice; we have eaten the fruit of lies. We have trusted in our own way; do not destroy us! Because of our great evil we appeal to the righteousness of Christ, for apart from Him we should be dashed in pieces and utterly cut off.

O great Son of David, we praise Your Name and bow with trembling, thankful hearts. Hasten Your glorious return! Amen (Hosea 10).

ost High Father,
Thank You that, when my husband was a child, You loved him, and out of Egypt You called Your son. Thank You for persisting, even when the more he was called, the more he went away and kept sacrificing to the gods of this world and burning offerings to self. Even so it was You who taught him to walk; You took him up by his arms, and now he knows that You healed him. Let him rejoice and sing for joy. For You led him with cords of kindness, with the bands of love, and You became to him as one who eases the yoke on his jaws, and You bent down to him and fed him.

O beloved, take care, and keep your soul diligently, lest you forget the things that your eyes have seen, and lest they depart from your heart all the days of your life.

Sovereign LORD, when his heart is bent on turning away from You, may Your compassion grow warm and tender. On account of Christ Jesus do not execute Your burning anger; for You are God and not a man, the Holy One in our midst, and because of Your great mercy do not come in wrath.

If he strays, roar like a lion, so that when You roar he will come trembling—trembling like a bird from Egypt. Then may he walk with You and remain faithful to the Holy One (Hosea 11 & Deuteronomy 4).

I had rather learn what some men really judge about their own justification from their prayers *than their writings.* ~John Owen

ORD God of hosts,

May my husband, by Your help, hold fast to love and justice, and wait continually for You. Keep him from incurring guilt and forsaking Christ. For if he does he shall be like the morning mist or like the dew that goes early away, like the chaff that swirls from the threshing floor or like smoke from a window. You are the LORD our God; we know no God but You, and besides You there is no savior. It was You who knew him in the wilderness, in the land of drought. But now, when he is filled, and his heart is lifted up, let him not forget You.

Even when he turns away from his Helper, do not destroy him, because of Christ. I thank You for His sacrifice on his behalf, so that You will not devour him and rip him open in Your wrath.

O beloved, bless the Name of Jesus, for He has ransomed you from the power of Sheol! He has redeemed you from Death. O Death, where are your plagues? O Sheol, where is your sting? The sting of death is sin, and the power of sin is the law. But thanks be to God, who gives us the victory through our Lord Jesus Christ.

LORD God, let not compassion be hidden from Your eyes toward him. Amen (Hosea 12, 13, I Corinthians 15).

ORD God of Israel,
Continue in faithful mercy toward my husband. Turn Your anger from him and love him freely. Be like the dew to him, causing him to blossom like the lily, and take root like the trees of Lebanon. Then his shoots shall spread out; his beauty shall be like the olive, and his fragrance like Lebanon. Let him dwell beneath Your shadow; may he flourish like the grain and blossom like the vine; make his fame be like the wine of Lebanon.

O beloved, what has our LORD God to do with idols? It is He who answers and looks after you. He is like an evergreen cypress; from Him comes your fruit.

Sovereign LORD, let him be wise and understand these things; give him discernment to know them; for Your ways are right, and the upright walk in them, but transgressors stumble in them (Hosea 14).

In God's commands to pray, we are compelled by the force of divine authority to come and drink of the living water, to receive bread from heaven, and to realize afresh moment by moment by moment that all that we long for, and everything that is good, is found in one and only one place: in God.
~Bruce Ware

ORD of Zion,

Thank You that through Christ my husband is washed; he is made clean; the evil of his deeds is removed from before Your eyes because He has borne his punishment. Assist him now to cease to do evil, learn to do good, seek justice, correct oppression, bring justice to the fatherless, plead the widow's cause.

Come now, beloved, let us reason together: though your sins were like scarlet, they are now white as snow; though they were red like crimson, they have now become like wool. Trust Christ for your righteousness! He is a great Savior.

Come, LORD God, and lead him up to Your mountain, to the house of the God of Jacob, that You may teach him Your ways and that he may walk in Your paths. O LORD, let him walk in Your light.

Let him stop regarding man in whose nostrils is breath, for of what account is he? Instead, give him more regard for Christ, so that on the day of the LORD he will not need to hide in the dust from before Your terror, and from the splendor of Your majesty. Prepare us together for that day, when the haughty looks of man shall be brought low, and the lofty pride of men shall be humbled, and You alone will be exalted (Isaiah 1 & 2).

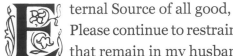ternal Source of all good,

Please continue to restrain the wicked inclinations that remain in my husband's heart. For if You do not, he will soon become haughty and walk with an outstretched neck, glancing wantonly with his eyes. Go on with Your work of making him holy, washing away his filth, and cleansing his bloodstains by a spirit of purging.

Thank You for loving him as a choice vineyard, and planting him with choice vines on a fertile hill. Now let him yield grapes, and not wild grapes.

O beloved, you are the LORD's pleasant planting. Therefore, do not feast with tambourine and flute and wine, and disregard the deeds of the LORD, or turn a blind eye to the work of His hands.

LORD of hosts, let him never be found lacking in the knowledge of You, so that he may not condemn himself to exile, hunger, and thirst. For before You man is humbled, and each one is brought low, and the eyes of the haughty are brought low. But You are exalted in justice, and You show Yourself holy in righteousness (Isaiah 3, 4, 5).

I have been benefited by praying for others; for by making an errand to God for them I have gotten something for myself.
~Samuel Rutherford

ORD of hosts,

Guard my husband from those who draw iniquity with cords of falsehood, who draw sin as with cart ropes. Protect him from those who call evil good and good evil, who put darkness for light and light for darkness, who put bitter for sweet and sweet for bitter! There are many who are wise in their own eyes, and shrewd in their own sight; let him not be found among them. Make him stand firm and humble in the midst of those who are heroes at drinking wine, who acquit the guilty for a bribe, and deprive the innocent of his right. For they have rejected Your law, and have despised the word of the Holy One of Israel. Therefore, their root will be as rottenness, and their blossom will go up like dust.

O beloved, sing with me the words of the seraphim. "Holy, holy, holy is the LORD of hosts; the whole earth is full of His glory!" Behold, through Christ your guilt is taken away, and your sin atoned for. Therefore, you can now rejoice when your eyes see the King, the LORD of hosts.

Help him to remain firm in faith, O LORD. For if he is not firm in faith, he will not be firm at all. And let him not fear what the world fears, nor be in dread. But You, O LORD of hosts—may he regard You as holy. May You be his fear, and may You be his dread. Amen (Isaiah 5, 6, 7, 8).

mniscient Father,

Thank You that my dearest husband who walked in darkness has seen a great light; he used to dwell in a land of deep darkness, but now on him light has shined. Please multiply his fruit; increase his joy; may he rejoice before You as with joy at the harvest, as those who are glad when they divide great spoil. For the yoke of his burden, and the staff for his shoulder, and the rod of his oppressor, You have broken as on the day of Midian. For to us a child was born, to him the Son was given; and the government is upon His shoulder, and His name is called Wonderful Counselor, Mighty God, Everlasting Father, Prince of Peace.

O beloved, let us adore our great Savior! Of the increase of His government and of peace there will be no end. He has established it and upholds it with justice and with righteousness from this time forth and forevermore.

O LORD of hosts, thank You that Your zeal has accomplished salvation for him through Christ. Amen (Isaiah 9).

In personal relationships, if we attempt to fake emotional intensity and put on an outward show of emotion that is not consistent with the feelings of our hearts, others involved will usually sense our hypocrisy at once and be put off by it. How much more is this true of God, who fully knows our hearts. Therefore, intensity and depth of emotional involvement in prayer should never be faked: we cannot fool God.
~Wayne Grudem

ajestic One,

In this day let my husband lean on You, the Holy One of Israel, in truth. Please continue to change him into the likeness of the shoot that came forth from the stump of Jesse. May Your Spirit rest upon him, the Spirit of wisdom and understanding, the Spirit of counsel and might, the Spirit of knowledge and the fear of the LORD. And let his delight be always in the fear of You. Clothe him with righteousness as the belt of his waist, and faithfulness as the belt of his loins.

I will give thanks to You, O LORD, for though You were once angry with him, Your anger turned away because of Christ, that You might comfort him.

O beloved, God is your salvation; trust, and do not be afraid; for the Lord GOD is your strength and your song, and He has become your salvation!

Therefore, O God, cause him to draw water from the wells of salvation with joy. And may he give thanks to You, call upon Your name, make known Your deeds among the peoples, and proclaim that Your name is exalted. May he sing praises to You, for You have done gloriously; let him make this known in all the earth. Let us shout together and sing for joy, for great in our midst are You, O Holy One of Israel (Isaiah 10, 11, 12).

Sovereign, eternal, unchangeable LORD, You are my God; I will exalt You; I will praise Your name, for You have done wonderful things, plans formed of old, faithful and sure. For You have made my husband; he is the work of Your hands. Let him glorify You; let him fear You. May You be to him a stronghold; a stronghold when he is needy and in distress, his shelter from the storm and his shade from the heat.

May he hope and long for the day when You will make for all peoples a feast of rich food, a feast of well-aged wine, of rich food full of marrow, of aged wine well refined.

O beloved, on that day He will swallow up death forever; and the Lord GOD will wipe away tears from all faces, and the reproach of His people He will take away from all the earth, for the LORD has spoken.

You are our God; we have waited for You, that You might save us. You are the LORD; together we have waited for You; let us be glad and rejoice in Your salvation. Keep my husband in perfect peace because his mind is stayed on You, because he trusts in You. Help him to trust in You forever, for You are an everlasting rock (Isaiah 25 & 26).

You should, in Tertullian's phrase, with a holy conspiracy, besiege heaven. ~Thomas Manton

O LORD my God, Please make level the path of my husband, for You make the way of the righteous level. In the path of Your judgments, O LORD, let him wait for You; may Your name and remembrance be the desire of his soul. Make his soul yearn for You in the night; cause his spirit within him to earnestly seek You. For when Your judgments are in the earth, the inhabitants of the world learn righteousness.

O LORD, ordain peace for him; do for him all his works. Even though other lords besides You may rule over him, let him bring Your name alone to remembrance.

You have made him a pleasant vineyard, a vineyard of wine; I will sing of him! Let him trust You, for You, the LORD, are his keeper; every moment You water him. You keep him night and day; may he lay hold of Your protection. In the days to come let him blossom and put forth shoots and fill the whole world with fruit. Amen (Isaiah 26 & 27).

ORD of power,
Please be to my beloved a crown of glory and a diadem of beauty. For You are the LORD of hosts, wonderful in counsel and excellent in wisdom.

Protect him from hypocrisy. May it never be that he draw near with his mouth and honor You with his lips, while his heart is far from You. Let his fear of You be genuine, and not a commandment taught by men.

O beloved, guard your heart, lest you turn things upside down and regard the Potter as the clay.

O LORD, keep him from saying of his Maker, "He did not make me"; or of You who formed him, "He has no understanding." Instead, let him be turned into a fruitful field. Out of his gloom and darkness, cause him to see and obtain fresh joy in You. May he exult in You, the Holy One of Israel, and no more be ashamed. Let him see the work of Your hands and sanctify Your name; let him sanctify the Holy One of Jacob and stand in awe of the God of Israel (Isaiah 28 & 29).

Just as God's Word must reform our theology, our ethics, and our practices, so also must it reform our praying. ~D.A. Carson

xalted Fountain of Grace,
May my husband find his strength in quietness and in trust, for You wait to be gracious to him. Therefore, exalt Yourself to show mercy to him. For You are a God of justice; blessed are all those who wait for You. Gather him into Your arms so that he will weep no more.

O beloved, He will surely be gracious to you at the sound of your cry. As soon as He hears it, He answers you.

Let him trust Your promise, O LORD, that though You give him the bread of adversity and the water of affliction, yet You will not hide Yourself forever, but his eyes shall see his Teacher. And may his ears hear a word behind him, saying, "This is the way, walk in it," when he turns to the right or when he turns to the left. Let him also defile his idols of the flesh, and scatter them as unclean things, saying to them, "Be gone!"

Cause his hope to remain rooted and steadfast in You when calamity overtakes him. For soon the light of the moon will be as the light of the sun, and the light of the sun will be sevenfold, as the light of seven days, in the day when You bind up the brokenness of Your people, and heal the wounds inflicted by Your blow. With Your burning anger devour his enemies, and give him a song as in the night when a holy feast is kept, and gladness of heart, as when one sets out to the sound of the flute to go to the mountain of the LORD, to the Rock of Israel. Cause Your majestic voice to be heard by him. Amen (Isaiah 30).

orker of wonders, Continue to make my husband righteous, so that he may have peace, quietness, and security forever. O LORD, be gracious to him; I wait for You. Be his arm every morning, his salvation in the time of trouble. For You are exalted, for You dwell on high; fill him with justice and righteousness, and be the stability of his days, abundance of salvation, wisdom, and knowledge; let the fear of You be his treasure. Arise, O LORD, lift Yourself up; be exalted in him.

Help him to become a man who walks righteously and speaks uprightly, who despises the gain of oppressions, who shakes his hands, lest they hold a bribe, who stops his ears from hearing of bloodshed and shuts his eyes from looking on evil. Then he will dwell on the heights; his place of defense will be the fortress of rocks; his bread will be given him; his water will be sure.

Let his eyes behold You in Your beauty. Be with him in majesty, for You are his judge; You are his lawgiver; You are his king; You will save him (Isaiah 32 & 33).

One cannot begin to face the real difficulties of the life of prayer and meditation unless one is first perfectly content to be a beginner and really experience himself as one who knows little or nothing and has a desperate need to learn the bare rudiments. Those who think they "know" from the beginning will never, in fact, come to know anything. ~Thomas Merton

Beautiful LORD,
Let my husband be glad as he looks to the day of the Son's return. May he rejoice and blossom like the crocus; let him blossom abundantly and rejoice with joy and singing. And may he long to see Your glory, the majesty of his God. Strengthen his weak hands, and make firm his feeble knees.

O beloved, be not anxious of heart. Be strong; fear not! Behold, your God will come with vengeance, with the recompense of God. He will come and save you. Then the eyes of the blind shall be opened, and the ears of the deaf unstopped; then shall the lame man leap like a deer, and the tongue of the mute sing for joy.

Prepare him, O LORD, to set foot on the great highway, which shall be called the Way of Holiness; for the unclean shall not pass over it. It shall belong to those who walk on the way; let him not go astray. Let him yearn for that day when the redeemed shall walk there, when the ransomed of the LORD shall return and come to Zion with singing. Everlasting joy shall be upon their heads; they shall obtain gladness and joy, and sorrow and sighing shall flee away (Isaiah 35).

God can pick sense out of a confused prayer. ~Richard Sibbes

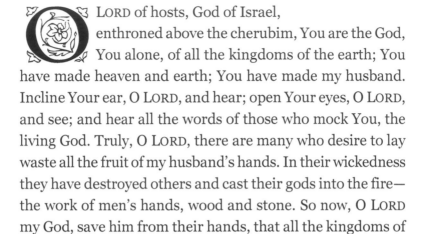

LORD of hosts, God of Israel, enthroned above the cherubim, You are the God, You alone, of all the kingdoms of the earth; You have made heaven and earth; You have made my husband. Incline Your ear, O LORD, and hear; open Your eyes, O LORD, and see; and hear all the words of those who mock You, the living God. Truly, O LORD, there are many who desire to lay waste all the fruit of my husband's hands. In their wickedness they have destroyed others and cast their gods into the fire—the work of men's hands, wood and stone. So now, O LORD my God, save him from their hands, that all the kingdoms of the earth may know that You alone are the LORD. Please defend him to save him, for Your own sake.

Please, O LORD, remember him and cause him to walk before You in faithfulness and with a whole heart, and to do what is good in Your sight. May he trust that it is for his welfare when he has great bitterness; let him praise You and hope for Your faithfulness.

O beloved, in love He has delivered your life from the pit of destruction, for He has cast all your sins behind His back.

Let him thank You, O LORD, as I do this day; let him make known to his children Your faithfulness. For it is You who will save us, and we will play music on stringed instruments all the days of our lives, at the house of the LORD (Isaiah 37 & 38).

Wonderful God, Comfort, comfort my dear husband. Speak tenderly to him and cry to him that his iniquity is pardoned, that because of Christ he has not received from Your hand double for all his sins. May he wait patiently for the day when Your glory shall be revealed, and all flesh shall see it together, for You have spoken.

O beloved, all flesh is grass, and all its beauty is like the flower of the field. The grass withers, the flower fades when the breath of the LORD blows on it; surely the people are grass. The grass withers, the flower fades, but the word of our God will stand forever.

Lord GOD, let him behold You coming with might; with Your arm ruling for You. Please tend him like a shepherd; gather him into Your arms; carry him in Your bosom, and gently lead him.

May he worship You as the only one who has measured the waters in the hollow of His hand and marked off the heavens with a span, enclosed the dust of the earth in a measure and weighed the mountains in scales and the hills in a balance. We praise You, for no man has directed Your Spirit or shown You his counsel. Amen (Isaiah 40).

As highly as Paul values marital obligations, he can envisage a couple self-consciously choosing not to have sex together for a while, so that the time they would have spent pleasing each other sexually will be devoted to prayer. That says something about Paul's valuation of prayer. ~D. A. Carson

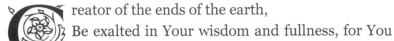

reator of the ends of the earth, Be exalted in Your wisdom and fullness, for You have never needed anyone. Whom did You consult, and who made You understand? Who taught You the path of justice, and taught You knowledge, and showed You the way of understanding? Behold, the nations are like a drop from a bucket, and are accounted as the dust on the scales; behold, You take up the coastlands like fine dust. Lebanon would not suffice for fuel, nor are its beasts enough for a burnt offering. All the nations are as nothing before You; they are accounted by You as less than nothing and emptiness.

Therefore, let my husband worship and adore Your greatness, taking comfort that You are powerful and lack nothing. O beloved, to whom then will you liken God, or what likeness compare with Him? You have known and heard, and it has been told you from the beginning, that it is He who sits above the circle of the earth, and its inhabitants are like grasshoppers; who stretches out the heavens like a curtain, and spreads them like a tent to dwell in; who brings princes to nothing, and makes the rulers of the earth as emptiness.

O Holy One, to whom then will we compare You, that You should be like him? Lift up our eyes on high to see: You created the stars—You who bring out their host by number, calling them all by name, by the greatness of Your might, and because You are strong in power not one is missing (Isaiah 40).

rue and only God,
May my husband never complain that his way is hidden from You, or that his right is disregarded by his God. Instead, assure him that You are the everlasting God, the Creator of the ends of the earth. Instill within him a steadfast confidence in You, for You do not faint or grow weary; Your understanding is unsearchable. Give power to him when he is faint, and when he has no might increase his strength. Even when he faints and becomes weary, when he falls exhausted, let him wait on You. For they who wait for You shall renew their strength; they shall mount up with wings like eagles; they shall run and not be weary; they shall walk and not faint.

Thank You for choosing him, for taking him from the pit, for calling him out of bondage, saying to him, "You are My servant, I have chosen you and not cast you off."

O beloved, fear not, for He is with you; be not dismayed, for He is your God; He will strengthen, He will help you, He will uphold you with His righteous right hand.

O LORD my God, hold his right hand, and say to him, "Fear not, I am the one who helps you" (Isaiah 40 & 41).

Intercession is more than specific: it is pondered: it requires us to bear on our heart the burden of those for whom we pray.
~George A. Buttrick

ing of Jacob, Defend my husband from all who are incensed against him; let them be put to shame and confounded; may those who strive against him be as nothing and perish. Let the evil ones who war against him be as nothing at all.

Fear not, beloved, you gift of God! He is the one who helps you; your Redeemer is the Holy One of Israel.

O LORD, let him rejoice in You; in the Holy One of Israel let him glory. When he is poor and needy and seeks for water, and there is none, and his tongue is parched with thirst, please answer him; O God of Israel, do not forsake him. Open rivers on the bare heights, and fountains in the midst of the valleys. Make the wilderness a pool of water, and the dry land springs of water for him. Put in his wilderness the cedar, the acacia, the myrtle, and the olive. Set in his desert the cypress, the plane and the pine together, that he may see and know, may consider and understand, that Your hand has done it, the Holy One of Israel has created it.

Increase his soul's delight in Your Servant, whom You uphold, Your chosen, just as Your soul delights in Him. May he hope in Him, for a bruised reed He will not break, and a faintly burning wick He will not quench; He will faithfully bring forth justice. Hasten the day of His return! Amen (Isaiah 41 & 42).

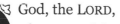 God, the LORD,
who created the heavens and stretched them out, who spread out the earth and what comes from it, who gives breath to the people on it and spirit to those who walk in it, reassure my husband that You are the LORD, and have called him in righteousness. Take him by the hand and keep him. Conform him to the image of Him who is given as a covenant for the people, a light for the nations, to open the eyes that are blind, to bring out the prisoners from the dungeon, from the prison those who sit in darkness.

O beloved, pursue Christ! Esteem Christ! Honor His Father, for He is the LORD; that is His name; His glory He gives to no other, nor His praise to carved idols.

Let him sing to You a new song, O LORD, Your praise from the end of the earth. Let him lift up his voice along with the sea, and all that fills it, the coastlands and their inhabitants, the desert and its cities. May he sing for joy, and shout from the top of the mountains. Let him give glory to You, and declare Your praise in the coastlands. For You go out like a mighty man, like a man of war You stir up Your zeal; You cry out, You shout aloud, You show Yourself mighty against Your foes.

Lead him in a way that he does not know, in paths that he has not known please guide him. Turn the darkness before him into light, the rough places into level ground. For these are the things that You do, and You will not forsake him (Isaiah 42).

Holy LORD,
Be pleased, for Your righteousness' sake, to magnify Your law and make it glorious through my husband. Be exalted, for You created him, You formed him. May he fear not, for You have redeemed him; You have called him by name, he is Yours. When he passes through the waters, please be with him; and through the rivers, let them not overwhelm him; when he walks through fire let him not be burned, and may the flame not consume him. For You are the LORD his God, the Holy One of Israel, his Savior.

O beloved, because you are precious in His eyes, and honored, and He loves you, He gives men in return for you, peoples in exchange for your life. Fear not, for He is with you. He is the LORD, and besides Him there is no savior.

Let him adore You as the LORD, his Redeemer, his Holy One, the Creator of Israel, his King. Give water to him in the wilderness, rivers when he is in the desert, to give drink to Your chosen son, the man whom You formed for Yourself that he might declare Your praise. Thank You that You are He who blots out his transgressions for Your own sake, and You will not remember his sins. For he is Your servant whom You have chosen; You made him and formed him from the womb. Help him, and let him not fear. Pour Your Spirit upon his offspring, and Your blessing on his descendants. Let them spring up among the grass like willows by flowing streams. May one say, "I am the LORD's,' and another write on his hand, "The LORD's," and name himself by the name of Israel (Isaiah 42, 43, 44).

ing and Redeemer of Israel,
Glory be to Your name, for You are the first and You are the last; besides You there is no god. Who is like You? Therefore, let my husband not fear, nor be afraid; for You declare what is to come, and what will happen. May he trust in You, for there is no god besides You, there is no Rock; I know not any. Let him remember that all who fashion idols are nothing, and the things they delight in do not profit, for he is Your servant; You formed him; he is Your servant; let him not be forgotten by You.

O beloved, He has blotted out your transgressions like a cloud and your sins like mist; cling to Him, for He has redeemed you!

Sing, O heavens, for the LORD has done it; shout, O depths of the earth; break forth into singing, O mountains, O forest, and every tree in it! For You, LORD, have redeemed my husband, and will be glorified in him. Through him be pleased to display Your beauty.

May he take comfort and rejoice in the knowledge that You formed him in the womb, that You are the LORD, who made all things, who alone stretched out the heavens, who spread out the earth by Yourself, who frustrates the signs of liars and makes fools of diviners, who turns wise men back and makes their knowledge foolish, who says to the deep, "Be dry; I will dry up your rivers." Let him love and fear You. Amen (Isaiah 44).

All progress in prayer is an answer to prayer—our own or another's. And all true prayer promotes its own progress and increases our power to pray. ~P. T. Forsyth

ORD God of Israel, who calls His people by name, I come before You on behalf of my dearest husband because You are the LORD, and there is no other, besides You there is no God. Please equip him to make known Your might, that people may know, from the rising of the sun and from the west, that there is none besides You; You are the LORD, and there is no other. May he tremble and rejoice at the truth that You form light and create darkness. Let him worship and bow down before You as the one who makes well-being and creates calamity. May he exalt You as the LORD who does all these things.

O beloved, praise and adore Him with me! For He made the earth and created man on it; it was His hands that stretched out the heavens, and He commanded all their host.

Stir him up, O LORD, in righteousness, and make all his ways level. May the wealthy and men of stature come to him, saying, "Surely God is in you, and there is no other, no god besides Him."

Many men make idols and go in confusion together. But I thank You that my husband is saved by You with everlasting salvation; he shall not be put to shame or confounded to all eternity. For You are the LORD and there is no other. You did not say to him, "Seek me in vain." You speak truth; You declare what is right (Isaiah 45).

God who hears prayer, Let my husband turn continually to You for his salvation. For You are God, and there is no other. Therefore let him say of You, "Only in the LORD are righteousness and strength." Thank You that in You he is justified and glories. Praise be to Your name, for he has been borne by You from before his birth, carried from the womb; even to his old age You are He, and to gray hairs You will carry him. You have made, and You will bear; You will carry and will save.

O beloved, remember with me that He is God, and there is no other; He is God, and there is none like Him, declaring the end from the beginning and from ancient times things not yet done, saying, "My counsel shall stand, and I will accomplish all my purpose."

Therefore, great LORD, may he trust the word that goes out from Your mouth in righteousness. Let him hope in You as the God who brings to pass what He speaks; who does what He has purposed. For Your name's sake be gracious to him, for the sake of Your praise make him walk in holiness, and do not cut him off. Refine him, and give him strength as You try him in the furnace of affliction. For Your own sake, for Your own sake, do this, for how should Your name be profaned? Your glory You will not give to another. Therefore magnify Yourself in him! Glorify Yourself through him! Use him to exalt the greatness of Your name. Amen (Isaiah 45, 46, 48).

y Redeemer,
Teach my husband to profit from uprightness, and lead him in the way he should go. Make him pay attention to Your commandments so that his peace will be like a river, and his righteousness like the waves of the sea; then let his offspring be like the sand, and his descendents like its grains; may their name never be cut off or destroyed from before You.

Now, even now I shout for joy, for You have redeemed him! Therefore do not let him thirst when You lead him through deserts; make water flow for him even from the rocks, so that his soul is satisfied.

Make his mouth like a sharp sword; in the shadow of Your hand please hide him; make him a polished arrow; in Your quiver hide him away.

O beloved, you are the LORD's servant, in whom He will be glorified and display His beauty. You have not labored in vain; you have not spent your strength for nothing. For surely your recompense is with your God.

I will praise You, O LORD, for You called him from the womb, from the body of his mother You named his name. You formed him from the womb to be Your servant, therefore may he be honored in Your eyes, and may You continually be his strength. Make him as a light for the nations, that Your salvation may reach to the ends of the earth. Let kings see and arise; may princes prostrate themselves; because of You, who are faithful, the Holy One of Israel, who has chosen him (Isaiah 48 & 49).

Ruler of heaven and earth, Please keep my husband. Answer him and help him; let him not hunger or thirst, and may neither scorching wind nor sun strike him. Have pity on him and lead him, and by springs of water guide him.

Sing for joy, O heavens, and exult, O earth; break forth, O mountains, into singing! For the LORD has comforted my beloved and will have compassion on his affliction.

I praise You that You have not forsaken him; You have not forgotten him. Even a woman may forget her nursing child, yet You will not forget my husband. Assure him of this, and let him know that You are the LORD; those who wait for You shall not be put to shame. Fight for him; contend with those who contend with him. Then all flesh shall know that You are the LORD his Savior, and his Redeemer, the Mighty One of Jacob (Isaiah 49).

The artless child is still the divine model for all of us. Prayer will increase in power and reality as we repudiate all pretense and learn to be utterly honest before God as well as before men.
~A. W. Tozer

Forgiving God,
Thank You that Your hand is not shortened, that it can redeem my dear husband. For by Your power and rebuke You dry up the sea, and make the rivers a desert.

Please give him the tongue of those who are taught, that he may know how to sustain with a word those who are weary. Morning by morning awaken him; awaken his ear to hear as those who are taught.

When he is struck and spit upon for Your namesake fill him with hope in You, the Lord GOD. For You will help him; therefore he will not be disgraced. Remind him that he will not be put to shame, for You who vindicate him are near.

Let him fear You and obey the voice of Your servant, Christ. And when he walks in darkness and has no light let him trust in Your name and rely on his God. Cause him to pursue righteousness and seek You. Make his wilderness like Eden, his desert like the garden of the LORD; may joy and gladness be found in him, thanksgiving and the voice of song (Isaiah 50 & 51).

Prayer is often represented as the great means of the Christian life. But it is no mere means, it is the great end of that life. It is, of course, not untrue to call it a means. It is so, especially at first. But at last it is truer to say that we live the Christian life in order to pray than that we pray in order to live the Christian life. ~P. T. Forsyth

ovely God,

Turn the attention of my husband to Yourself. Let him give ear to the law that has gone out from You, to the justice that You have set for a light to the peoples. May Your righteousness draw near to him, let Your salvation go out to him; make him hope for You, and for Your arm let him wait. Lift up his eyes to the heavens, and cause him to look at the earth beneath and see that the heavens vanish like smoke, the earth will wear out like a garment, and they who dwell in it will die in like manner. But remind him that Your salvation will be forever, and Your righteousness will never be dismayed.

Listen to Him, O beloved, you who know righteousness; for He says, "Fear not the reproach of man, nor be dismayed at their revilings. For the moth will eat them up like a garment, and the worm will eat them like wool; but My righteousness will be forever, and My salvation to all generations."

Awake, awake, put on strength, O arm of the LORD; awake, as in days of old, the generations of long ago, and defend my husband. You have ransomed him, therefore let him come into Your presence with singing; crown his head with everlasting joy; grant him gladness and joy, so that sorrow and sighing shall flee away.

Teach him to not be afraid of man who dies, of the son of man who is made like grass, for You, You are He who comforts him. Let him take confidence in You, his Maker, who stretched out the heavens and laid the foundations of the earth, and may he fear not the oppressors who set themselves up to destroy (Isaiah 51).

ord of the oceans, who stirs up the sea so that its waves roar, please put Your words in my husband's mouth and cover him in the shadow of Your hand. For You are the LORD of hosts, who established the heavens and laid the foundations of the earth, and say to him, "You are My son."

Thank You for awakening him from the slumber of death, for clothing him with strength and beautiful garments. For he was sold for nothing, and You have redeemed him without money. Therefore make his feet beautiful upon the mountains, as one who brings good news, who publishes peace, who brings good news of happiness, who publishes salvation, who says, "My God reigns." Let him lift up his voice with me, so that together we may sing for joy, and eye to eye await the return of Your Son.

O beloved, let us break forth together into singing, for the LORD has comforted His people; He has redeemed even us! The LORD has bared His holy arm before the eyes of all the nations, and all the ends of the earth shall see the salvation of our God.

LORD, please go always before him; O God of Israel, be his rear guard. Amen (Isaiah 51 & 52).

When our awareness of the greatness of God and the gospel is dim, our prayer lives will be small. The less we think of the nature and character of God, and the less we are reminded of what Jesus did for us on the Cross, the less we want to pray.
~Donald S. Whitney

My Father and my God,

Grow within the heart of my husband a deep esteem for Him who has borne his griefs and carried his sorrows, who was wounded for his transgressions and crushed for his iniquities. May he treasure Him increasingly, desire Him more fervently, for upon Him was the chastisement that brought him peace, and with His stripes he is healed.

Let him love and cherish Him as the One stricken for his transgression. May he praise You with trembling for crushing Him so that he could be accounted righteous. Stir up gratitude within him for His sacrifice, for bearing his iniquities, pouring out His soul to death, and for making intercession for him.

Sing, O beloved! Break forth into singing and cry aloud! For you have been reconciled to your Maker and Husband, to the LORD of hosts; the Holy of One of Israel is your Redeemer! (Isaiah 53 & 54).

od of the whole earth, Do not hide Your beautiful face from my husband or be angry with him, but with everlasting love have compassion on him. Even though the mountains may depart and the hills be removed, let not Your steadfast love depart from him, and do not remove Your covenant of peace, but continue to have compassion on him.

O beloved, although you may be afflicted and storm-tossed, take comfort in His word! For behold, He will set your stones in antimony, and lay your foundations with sapphires. He will wall you in with precious stones.

LORD, bless him, and may all his children be taught by You, and let the peace of his children be great. Establish him in righteousness; keep him far from oppression and fear. Protect him from terror; may it not come near him. I commit him to Your hand, for You guard him so that no weapon that is fashioned against him shall succeed (Isaiah 54).

Meditation is a middle sort of duty between the word and prayer, and hath respect to both. The word feedeth meditation, and meditation feedeth prayer. These duties must always go hand in hand; meditation must follow hearing and precede prayer. To hear and not to meditate is unfruitful. We may hear and hear, but it is like putting a thing into a bag with holes.... It is rashness to pray and not to meditate. What we take in by the word we digest by meditation and let out by prayer. These three duties must be ordered that one may not jostle out the other. Men are barren, dry, and sapless in their prayers for want of exercising themselves in holy thoughts. ~ Thomas Manton

ompassionate LORD,

When my husband thirsts, draw him to the waters, draw him to Yourself. Keep him from spending his money for that which is not bread, and his labor for that which does not satisfy. Instead, make him listen diligently to You, and eat what is good, and delight himself in rich food—wine and milk without price. Incline his ear, and let him come to You; may he hear, that his soul may live, because of Your everlasting covenant of steadfast, sure love.

O beloved, seek the LORD while He may be found; call upon Him while He is near! Let us forsake our wicked ways and our unrighteous thoughts; and let us turn to the LORD, that He may have compassion on us, and to our God, for He will abundantly pardon.

Holy One of Israel, we bow together before You, for Your thoughts are not our thoughts, neither are Your ways our ways. We worship and exalt You, for as the heavens are higher than the earth, so are Your ways higher than our ways and Your thoughts than our thoughts. Amen (Isaiah 55).

God who is high and lifted up, Be pleased to fill my husband with joy and lead him forth in peace. May he keep justice, and do righteousness, for Your salvation has come, and Your deliverance is revealed. Keep his hand from doing any evil, and make him hold on to righteousness.

Thank You for saving him; for giving him an everlasting name that shall not be cut off. Let the mountains and the hills break forth into singing, and all the trees of the field clap their hands! For You have made a name for Yourself; You have redeemed him! Make him joyful in Your house of prayer.

Please protect him from blind watchmen without knowledge, from shepherds who have no understanding. Revive his spirit when he is lowly, and revive his heart when he is contrite. May he seek You daily and delight to know Your ways; let him delight to draw near to You. And when he fasts, may it not be merely to quarrel and pursue his own business. But cause him to fast as You choose: to loose the bonds of wickedness, to undo the straps of the yoke, to let the oppressed go free, to share his bread with the hungry, to bring the homeless poor into his house, and to clothe the naked. Then may his light break forth like the dawn, and make righteousness go before him, with Your glory as his rear guard (Isaiah 55, 56, 58).

A chief object of all prayer is to bring us to God....
The chief failure of prayer is its cessation. ~P. T. Forsyth

ord who inhabits eternity,

When I call to You, please answer. I cry out to You on behalf of my dearest husband. Keep him from speaking wickedness. But rather, may he pour himself out for the hungry and satisfy the desire of the afflicted, for then shall his light rise in the darkness and his gloom be as the noonday. Guide him continually and satisfy his desire in scorched places and make his bones strong; may he be like a watered garden, like a spring of water, whose waters do not fail. Let him take delight in You; feed him with the heritage of Jacob.

O beloved, arise, shine, for your light has come, and the glory of the LORD has risen upon you. Although darkness once covered you, now the LORD has risen upon you, and His glory is seen upon you. And nations shall come to your light, and kings to the brightness of Christ in you!

LORD God, may peoples see him and be radiant; let their hearts thrill and exult because of the abundance of his joy in Christ. Make him declare the good news—the praises of Christ. Cause Your servant to shine so that the coastlands will hope for You, for the name of the LORD his God, and for the Holy One of Israel, because You have made him Yours (Isaiah 58 & 60).

O God whose name is Holy, In Your favor be pleased to have mercy on my husband. Make him majestic forever, and a joy to every age, so that all may know that You, the LORD, are his Savior and his Redeemer, the Mighty One of Jacob. Make his overseers peace and his taskmasters righteousness. May his clothing be called Salvation, and the gates to his house Praise.

O beloved, trust in the LORD, and He will be your everlasting light, and your God will be your glory! Seek His face, and He will be your strength.

LORD, let him hope in You as his everlasting light. Clothe him with righteousness that You may be glorified. Use him to display Your beauty.

Please comfort him when he mourns; give him the oil of gladness instead of mourning, the garment of praise instead of a faint spirit; that he may be called an oak of righteousness, the planting of the LORD, that You may be glorified. Let him greatly rejoice in You; let his soul exult in his God, for You have clothed him with the garments of salvation; You have covered him with the robe of righteousness, as a bride adorns herself with her jewels. As the earth brings forth its sprouts, and as a garden causes what is sown in it to sprout up, so cause righteousness and praise to sprout up before him. Amen (Isaiah 60 & 61).

Even as the moon influences the tides of the sea, even so does prayer...influence the tides of godliness. ~Charles Spurgeon

uthor of all existence,

For my husband's sake do not keep silent, and for his sake do not be quiet, until his righteousness goes forth as brightness, and his salvation as a burning torch. Let men see his righteousness, and women his glory, because You have called him by a new name that Your mouth has given. May he be as a crown of beauty in Your hand, and a royal diadem in the hand of his God. Let him be called My Delight Is in Him, for You delight in Your servant. Fill him with the joyful knowledge that You take pleasure in him, that as the bridegroom rejoices over the bride, so You rejoice over him. Please establish him and make him a praise in the earth. Let those who eat the grain and drink the wine of his house praise the LORD, and exult in Your holiness.

O beloved, behold, your salvation has come; behold, His reward is Himself! Rejoice! For you are numbered among The Holy People, The Redeemed of the LORD; and you are called Sought Out, A Man Not Forsaken.

O Mighty One, help him to put his hope in You—You who are splendid in Your apparel, marching in the greatness of Your strength, speaking in righteousness, mighty to save. Thank You for sparing his lifeblood and bringing to him salvation by Your powerful arm. Thank You, that when he deserved to be trod in Your anger and trampled in Your wrath, You gave Christ to bear his punishment! We bless His name together, for He is our joy and our salvation (Isaiah 62 & 63).

Source of all blessedness, Let my husband be a man who recounts Your steadfast love, Your praises, according to all that You have given us, and the great goodness to our house that You have granted us according to Your compassion, according to the abundance of Your steadfast love. Thank You for becoming his Savior; that in Your love and in Your pity You have redeemed him, and lifted him up and carried him. Please continue to lead him, to make for Yourself a glorious name.

O beloved, it is my joy once again to remind you that He is your Father, though Abraham does not know you; He, the LORD, is your Father, your Redeemer from of old is His name!

O LORD, do not make him wander from Your ways and harden his heart, so that he fears You not. Keep him, and let him wait for You. For from of old no one has heard or perceived by the ear, no eye has seen a God besides You, who acts for those who wait for Him. You meet him who joyfully works righteousness—him who remembers Your ways. Therefore may he present himself to You as a joyful servant of righteousness, remembering the ways of his God (Isaiah 63 & 64).

A day without prayer is a boast against God. ~Owen Carr

Praiseworthy LORD,
I am glad and rejoice forever in my husband whom You have created; for behold, You made his face to be my joy, and his presence to be my gladness. Give him the assurance that You also rejoice in him and are glad in Your people.

Let him live by faith, hoping for the day when You create a new heavens and a new earth—when the sound of weeping and the cry of distress shall be heard no more, when Your chosen shall not labor in vain or bear children for calamity, when the wolf and the lamb shall graze together.

Guard him from the subtle deceitfulness of pride; help him to fight against arrogance. For this is the one to whom You will look: he who is humble and contrite in spirit and trembles at Your word.

Let him see Your glory and declare it among the nations, so that all flesh may know that You are the LORD and come to worship before You (Isaiah 65 & 66).

nfinitely worthy LORD, I will sing to You, for You have done glorious things; You have made my husband, You made Yourself his strength and his song, and You have become his salvation! You are my God, and I will praise You for him; You are the God of Jacob, and I will exalt You. Your right hand, O LORD, glorious in power, Your right hand, O LORD, shatters his enemies. In the greatness of Your majesty You overthrow his adversaries; You send out Your fury; it consumes them like stubble.

Who is like You, O LORD, among the gods? Who is like You, majestic in holiness, awesome in glorious deeds, doing wonders? You have led in Your steadfast love my husband whom You have redeemed; You have guided him by Your strength to Your holy abode. You alone will reign forever and ever.

I will sing to You, for You have triumphed gloriously over his enemies; You will guard and defend him, for You have become his salvation! (Exodus 15).

What is the reason that some believers are so much brighter and holier than others? I believe the difference, nineteen cases out of twenty, arises from different habits about private prayer. I believe that those who are not eminently holy pray little, and those who are eminently holy pray much. ~J. C. Ryle

ost blessed LORD, Let my husband be a man who proclaims Your name and ascribes greatness to his God. For You are the Rock, whose work is perfect, for all Your ways are justice. A God of faithfulness and without iniquity, just and upright are You.

Keep him from becoming unmindful of the Rock that bore him, from forgetting the God who gave him birth. But make him remember and rejoice that You, even You, are his help, and there is no god beside You. You kill and You make alive; You wound and You heal; and there is none that can deliver out of Your hand.

Rejoice with Him, O beloved; bow down to Him, for He avenges the blood of His children and takes vengeance on His adversaries.

Most High God, let him dwell in safety; surround him all day long, and dwell between his shoulders. May he be blessed by You with favor, and be full of the blessing of the LORD. For there is none like You, who rides through the heavens to his help, through the skies in Your majesty. Be his dwelling place, and keep Your everlasting arms underneath him. Amen (Deuteronomy 32 & 33).

O Lord God, Who am I, and what is my house, that You have given me such a husband? And yet this was a small thing in Your eyes, O Lord GOD. According to Your own heart You have brought him to me, to make Your servant know Your abundant goodness. Therefore You are great, O LORD God. For there is none like You, and there is no God besides You.

And who is like my husband? I praise You that he is Your child, one of the men on earth whom You went to redeem to be Your son, making Yourself a name and doing for him great and awesome things. You established him for Yourself to be Yours forever. And You, O LORD, became his God.

And now, O LORD God, let Your name be magnified forever through him. Let him say, "The LORD of hosts is God over His people." Your promises are sure; You are his God, therefore Your servant has found courage to pray this prayer to You. May it please You to bless the husband of Your servant, so that he may continue forever before You. For only with Your blessing shall the husband of Your servant be blessed forever (II Samuel 7).

The great fault of the children of God is, they do not continue in prayer; they do not go on praying; they do not persevere. *If they desire anything for God's glory, they should pray until they get it. Oh, how good, and kind, and gracious, and condescending is the One with Whom we have to do! He has given me, unworthy as I am, immeasurably above all I had asked or thought!*
~George Mueller

ORD of Thunder,

Please be my dear husband's rock and his fortress and his deliverer, his God, his rock, in whom he takes refuge, his shield, and the horn of his salvation, his stronghold and his refuge, his savior; save him from violence. I call upon You, who are worthy to be praised, to plead for his perseverance.

When the waves of death encompass him, when the torrents of destruction assail him, let him hope in You. When the cords of Sheol entangle him, when the snares of death confront him, in his distress let him call upon You; may he call to his God. Hear his voice, and may his cry come to Your ears. Send from on high and take hold of him; draw him out of many waters. Rescue him and bring him out into a broad place; rescue him because You delight in him.

Enable him to keep Your ways and let him not wickedly depart from his God. May all Your rules be before him, and from Your statutes may he not turn aside. Make him blameless before You, and help him to keep himself from guilt. Mold him into a merciful, pure man, for with the merciful You show Yourself merciful; with the blameless man You show Yourself blameless; with the purified You deal purely, and with the crooked You make Yourself seem tortuous (II Samuel 22).

avior of a humble people, Be my husband's lamp, O LORD, and lighten his darkness. Lead him in Your way, for Your way is perfect; Your word proves true; be a shield for him as he takes refuge in You. For who is God but You? And who is a rock, except You? Therefore please be his strong refuge and make his way blameless. Make his feet like the feet of a deer and set him securely on the heights. Train his hands for war, so that he may use the shield of Your salvation.

By Your gentleness make him great. Give a wide place for his steps under him, and let his feet not slip. Equip him with strength for battle; make the evil that rises against him sink under him.

O beloved, the LORD lives, and blessed be our rock, and exalted be our God, the rock of our salvation!

For this we will praise You, O LORD, among the nations, and sing praises to Your name! Bring great salvation to my husband, and show steadfast love to him forever (II Samuel 22).

The prayerless spirit saps a people's moral strength because it blunts their thought and conviction of the Holy. It must be so if prayer is such a moral blessing and such a shaping power, if it pass, by its nature, from the vague volume and passion of devotion to formed petition and effort. Prayerlessness is an injustice and a damage to our own soul, and therefore to its history, both in what we do and what we think. The root of all deadly heresy is prayerlessness. ~P. T. Forsyth

od of Jacob,
Raise up my husband to live in the fear of You, so that he may dawn on his children like the morning light, like the sun shining forth on a cloudless morning, like rain that makes grass to sprout from the earth.

Thank You that You have shown great and steadfast love to him, and have caused him to walk before You in faithfulness, in righteousness, and in uprightness of heart toward You. Please keep for him this great and steadfast love.

Give him an understanding mind that he may discern between good and evil. Grant him a wise and discerning mind, so that he may walk in Your ways, keeping Your statutes and Your commandments. For there is no God like You, O LORD, in heaven above or on earth beneath, keeping covenant and showing steadfast love to Your servants who walk before You with all their heart. Behold, heaven and the highest heaven cannot contain You, yet have regard to the prayer of Your servant and his plea, O LORD, my God, listening to the cry and to the prayer that Your servant prays before You this day on behalf of her husband. Let him fear You all the days that he lives, and may he shine forth the greatness of Your name, Your mighty hand, and Your outstretched arm (II Samuel 23, I Kings 3, 8).

There are many good resources for learning how to pray, but the best way to learn how to pray is to pray. ~Donald Whitney

Rock of Israel,
There is no God like You, in heaven above or on earth beneath, keeping covenant and showing steadfast love to Your servants who walk before You with all their heart. Therefore I ask that You would incline the heart of my dearest husband to walk in Your ways, keeping Your statutes. Keep him in the way everlasting; let him pay close attention to his way, to walk before You as David walked before You. Listen to the plea of Your servant when I pray for him; hear from heaven and teach him the good way in which he should walk, and rain grace upon him that he may fear You all the days of his life.

Let Your eyes be open to his pleas, giving ear to him whenever he calls You. For You chose him from among all the people of the earth to be Your heritage.

Blessed are You, O LORD, who has given rest to my husband. Not one word has failed of all Your good promise, which You spoke to Moses Your servant, which is his in Christ Jesus! Be with him, and do not leave him or forsake him, that You may incline his heart to Yourself, to walk in all Your ways and to keep Your commandments, Your statutes, and Your rules. Maintain his cause, that all the peoples of the earth may know that the LORD is God; there is no other. Let his heart therefore be wholly true to You our God, walking in Your statutes and keeping Your commandments (I Kings 8).

O Lord the God of Israel, Who is enthroned above the cherubim, You are the God, You alone, of all the kingdoms of the earth; You have made heaven and earth. Incline Your ear, O LORD, and hear; open Your eyes, O LORD, and see; and hear the words of my prayer on behalf of my husband.

Let him give thanks to You; let him call upon Your name and make known Your deeds among the peoples! May he sing to You; let him sing praises to You and tell of all Your wonderful works! Cause him to glory in Your holy name; let his heart seek You and rejoice!

O beloved, chosen of Jacob, seek the LORD and His strength; seek His presence continually! Remember the wondrous works that He has done, His miracles and the judgments He uttered.

LORD God, help him to remember Your covenant forever, the word that You commanded, for a thousand generations, the covenant that You made with Abraham. Let him sing to You with all the earth and tell of Your salvation from day to day! May he declare Your glory among the nations, Your marvelous works among all the peoples! For great are You, O LORD, and greatly to be praised, and You are to be held in awe above all gods. For all the gods of the peoples are idols, but You made the heavens. Splendor and majesty are before You; strength and joy are in Your place (II Kings 19 & I Chronicles 16).

G od of my salvation, Please increase my husband's desire to ascribe to You glory and strength—to ascribe to You the glory due Your name and come humbly before You! Let him worship You in the splendor of holiness, trembling before You with joy. Let him be glad with the heavens, and rejoice with the earth, and let him say among the nations, "The LORD reigns!" Let him roar with the sea, and all that fills it; let him exult with the field, and everything in it! Then make him sing for joy with the trees of the forest before You, for You come to judge the earth.

O beloved, give thanks to the LORD, for He is good; for His steadfast love endures forever.

Keep him to the end, O God of our salvation, and deliver him from among the nations, that he may give thanks to Your holy name, and glory in Your praise. For blessed are You, the God of Israel, from everlasting to everlasting! Amen. Praise the LORD! (I Chronicles 16).

The opposite of planning is the rut. If you don't plan a vacation you will probably stay home and watch TV. The natural, unplanned flow of spiritual life sinks to the lowest ebb of vitality. There is a race to be run and a fight to be fought. If you want renewal in your life of prayer you must plan to see it.
~John Piper.

ord of all being,
Let Your eyes be open and Your ears attentive to the prayer of Your servant. And now arise, O LORD, and go to him. Clothe him with salvation, and make him rejoice in Your goodness. O LORD God, do not turn away the face of Your anointed one! Remember Your steadfast love for my husband, Your servant. Let him worship You and give thanks to You, saying, "For He is good, for His steadfast love endures forever."

May he continually humble himself, and pray and seek Your face and turn from wicked ways. Open Your eyes and let Your ears be attentive to him, for You have chosen and consecrated him that Your name may be exalted forever. Let him praise You as the God of heaven, who rules over all the kingdoms of the nations—as the God in whose hand are power and might, so that none is able to withstand You. May he give thanks to You, for Your steadfast love endures forever (II Chronicles 6 & 20).

My God, the great, the mighty, and the awesome God,

O that my husband would delight himself in Your great goodness! Thank You that even when he forgets You and strays from Your commandments, in Your great mercies You do not make an end of him or forsake him, for You are a gracious and merciful God.

When hardships befall him, let them not seem little to You; when he cries to You hear from heaven and deliver him according to Your mercies.

Be exalted in Your grace, for although we have acted wickedly, You have dealt faithfully.

Let him not boast in his wisdom, nor in his might, nor in his riches, but let him boast in this: that he understands and knows You, that You are the LORD who practices steadfast love, and justice, and righteousness in the earth. For in these things You delight.

There is none like You, O LORD; You are great, and Your name is great in might. May he fear You, O King of the nations. For this is Your due; for among all the wise ones of the nations and in all their kingdoms there is none like You (Nehemiah 9, Jeremiah 9 & 10).

As it is the business of tailors to make clothes and of cobblers to mend shoes, so it is the business of Christians to pray.
~Martin Luther

ternal God,

Let my husband rejoice in the Word, through whom all things were made. May he seek life only in Him.

Praise be to Your name for causing him to receive Him and believe on His name, for giving him the right to become Your child. Open his eyes to the glory of the Word, the glory of Your only Son, full of grace and truth. From His fullness let him receive grace upon grace—the grace and truth that come through Jesus Christ. Help him to do what is true and come to the light, so that it may be clearly seen that his deeds have been carried out in You.

Help him not to judge by appearances, but instead to judge with right judgment. And when he thirsts, let him go to Christ and drink. Let him follow closely after Him always, so that he will not walk in darkness, but will have the light of life. Make him abide in His word as a true disciple so that he may know the truth and be set free by it (John 1 & 8).

reat Life-Giver,

May my husband never faint in following after his Shepherd's voice. Let Christ go before him and lead him, calling him by name and wooing him with His words.

Let him flee from the stranger, from the thief, and from the robber, for he does not know their voice.

I praise You that he has entered by Your Son into salvation and plentiful pasture. May he have life and have it abundantly in Him, for that is why He came. Let him trust Him always as his good Shepherd who lays down His life for sheep like him.

Enable him to shepherd me as Christ does, to lay his own life down for me, to guard and guide me diligently. May he never be like the hired hand who sees the wolf coming and leaves me and flees.

O beloved, trust Christ as your Shepherd! For His Father, who has given you to Him, is greater than all, and no one is able to snatch you out of Your Father's hand. And Christ and the Father are one (John 10).

Nothing would do more to cure us of a belief in our own wisdom than the granting of some of our eager prayers. And nothing could humiliate us more than to have God say when the fulfillment of our desire brought leanness to our souls, "Well, you would have it." It is what He has said to many. But He has said more, "My grace is sufficient for thee." ~P. T. Forsyth

Almighty Father,

Stir within my dear husband a stronger desire to glorify the Son of Man. Let him seek to glorify Him even in his death. For unless a grain of wheat falls into the earth and dies, it remains alone; but if it dies, it bears much fruit. And my desire is that he bear much fruit for the splendor of Your name. Therefore let him not love his life and so lose it, but help him to hate his life in this world so that he may keep it for eternal life. May he serve Christ and follow Christ, for then You will honor him.

Even in this very hour, Father, glorify Your name in him. Draw him to Yourself and let Christ always be his light, that he may not walk in darkness. Thank You that he has believed in the light and has become a son of light. I praise You that You did not blind his eyes or harden his heart so that he could not believe. But in grace You shone into his soul and made him to love the glory that comes from You more than the glory that comes from man (John 12).

F ather of our Lord and Teacher, Help my husband and me to persevere in washing one another's feet in all humility and joy. For Christ has given us an example, that we should also do as He has done to us. Assist us to do what we know as servants, for a servant is not greater than his master.

Please deliver my husband from the treachery that still indwells him, for if You remove Your hand of grace he will surely betray Your Son. O spare him that dreadful end! Keep him faithful and steadfast in Jesus all his days, so that He may be glorified, and You may be glorified in Him.

Cause us to grow in love for one another—to strive wholeheartedly to love each other just as Christ has loved us, so that all people will know that we are His disciples, if we have love for one another.

O beloved, let not your heart be troubled! Believe in God; believe also in Christ.

Father, fill him afresh with hope for the time when Your Son will come again and will take him to Himself, that where He is he may be also (John 13 & 14).

Prayer is a special exercise of faith. Faith makes the prayer acceptable because it believes that either the prayer will be answered, or that something better will be given instead.
~Martin Luther

uthor of Pleasure,

All thanks and praise belong to You for showing my husband the way to Yourself, which is through Jesus alone. Blessed be Your glorious name for revealing Christ to him as the way, and the truth, and the life! May he grow to know Him better today than he did yesterday, which is to know You, His Father. I ask this only in Your Son's name, that You may be glorified in Him.

Create within him deeper love for Christ, and let this love constrain him to keep His commandments. Thank You for giving him another Helper to be with him forever, even the Spirit of truth, whom the world cannot receive, because it neither sees Him nor knows Him. Let him sing praise to You, for Your Spirit dwells in him.

O beloved, do not despair, for Christ has not left us as orphans; He will come to us.

Father, may he love Christ and keep His words. By Your Holy Spirit, teach him all things and bring to his remembrance all that Christ has spoken. Grant His peace to him. Amen (John 14).

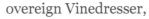

Sovereign Vinedresser,

Let not my husband's heart be troubled, neither let it be afraid. Remind him that Christ is mighty to save, and You will not leave him or forsake him. Help him to do as You have commanded him, so that the world may know that he loves You.

Please make him a branch that bears fruit because he abides in the vine, which is Christ. Prune him, that he may bear more fruit. Preserve him as one who abides in Christ and He in him, so that he bears much fruit, for apart from Christ he can do nothing.

O beloved, let us abide always in Jesus, with His words abiding in us. For then, when we ask whatever we wish, it will be done for us.

Father, glorify Yourself by making him bear much fruit, and so proving him to be Christ's disciple. May he abide in His love, for as You have loved Him, so has He loved him. Cause him to keep His commandments, for then he will abide in His love, just as He abides in Your love by keeping Your commandments.

Come quickly, Lord Jesus. Amen (John 14 & 15).

Humbly I asked of God to give me joy,
To crown my life with blossoms of delight;
I pled for happiness without alloy,
Desiring that my pathway should be bright;
Prayerfully I sought these blessings to attain, —
And now I thank him that he gave me pain....

For with the pain and sorrow came to me
A dower of tenderness in act and thought;
And with the failure came a sympathy,
An insight that success had never bought.
Father, I had been foolish and unblest
If thou had granted me my blind request!

~L. M. Montgomery

Electing God,
Thank You for choosing my husband and appointing him that he should go and bear fruit and that his fruit should abide. How gracious You are to call him Your friend! Fill him with love for his brothers and sisters in Christ, and for me. And fill me with fresh, fervent, bright, divinely-wrought love for him.

If the world hates him, remind him that it hated Christ before it hated him. Prepare him to expect the world's hatred, for You chose him out of the world and he is no longer of the world. Help him to remember the word spoken by Christ: "A servant is not greater than his master," so that he will not be surprised or lose heart when persecution comes.

Let him persevere in bearing witness about Your glorious Son and enable him to do so by Your wonderful Helper, the Spirit of truth, who proceeds from You. May he herald the name of Jesus with boldness and joy.

In the midst of persecution, Father, keep him from falling away! May his heart not falter in unbelief (John 15).

agnificent Father,
Now that Your Spirit of truth has come, let Him guide my husband into all the truth. May He glorify the Son by taking what is Christ's and declaring it to him. When he is sorrowful, turn his sorrow into joy. Fill him with hope that he will see Christ again soon, and then his heart will rejoice and no one will take his joy from him. Give him confidence to ask things of You in the name of Christ, for then he will receive, that his joy may be full. Imbue his soul with joy in Jesus! Cause him to listen to His words, that in Him he may have peace.

O beloved, in the world you will have tribulation. But take heart; Christ has overcome the world!

Father, grant him to know You, the only true God, and Jesus Christ more deeply, for that is eternal life. Enable him to glorify You on earth and accomplish the work that You have given him to do. Holy Father, keep us in Your name, that we may be one, even as You and Christ are one. Guard him so that he may never be lost. Open his ears to the words spoken by Your Son that he may have His joy fulfilled in himself. Thank You for giving us Your word through Christ! Amen (John 16 & 17).

O what peace we often forfeit,
O what needless pain we bear,
All because we do not carry
Everything to God in prayer!
~Joseph Scriven

od and Father of my Lord Jesus Christ, Praise be to Your name because You have blessed my dear husband in Christ with every spiritual blessing in the heavenly places, even as You chose him in Him before the foundation of the world, that he should be holy and blameless before You. Please continue to sanctify him by the love with which You predestined him for adoption through Jesus Christ, according to the purpose of Your will, to the praise of Your glorious grace, with which You have blessed him in the Beloved. Worthy is He! How beautiful is Your Son! Let His name be exalted! For in Him he has redemption through His blood, the forgiveness of his trespasses, according to the riches of Your grace, which You lavished on him, in all wisdom and insight.

O beloved, let us laud His name together for His rich and lavish grace toward us! For in Christ we have obtained an inheritance, having been predestined according to the purpose of Him who works all things according to the counsel of His will, so that we who hope in Christ might be to the praise of His glory!

Father, remind him of his former state as a child of wrath by nature, like the rest of mankind, when he was dead in his trespasses and sins. Remind him of this so that he will rejoice afresh that You, being rich in mercy, because of the great love with which You loved him, even when he was dead in his trespasses, made him alive with Christ and saved him by grace. Continue showing him the immeasurable riches of Your grace in kindness toward him in Christ Jesus. Amen (Ephesians 1 & 2).

ighty God,

Thank You for saving my husband by pure grace, so that he cannot boast as if it were his own doing, for his salvation is a gift of You and not a result of works. I praise Your name alone for the inestimable treasure that I have in him, because he is Your workmanship, created in Christ Jesus for good works. Therefore assist him to walk in the good works which You prepared beforehand for him.

Remind him constantly that he was at one time separated from Christ, having no hope and without God in the world. Remind him, so that he may rejoice continually that now in Christ Jesus he has been brought near by His blood. Fill him with the confidence that comes from knowing that Christ Himself is his peace—that He has reconciled him to You through the cross. Let him sing for joy anew because He has broken down the dividing wall of hostility between him and You—the one true and holy God.

In Christ please continue building us together into a dwelling place for Yourself by the Spirit. Amen (Ephesians 2).

No tongue can express, no mind can reach, the heavenly placidness and soul-satisfying delight which are intimated in these words [Eph 2:18]. To come to God as a Father, through Christ, by the help and assistance of the Holy Spirit, revealing him as a Father unto us, and enabling us to go to him as a Father, how full of sweetness and satisfaction is it!
~John Bunyan

od of revealed mystery, O that my husband would be granted insight into the mystery of Christ by Your Spirit! Give him more and more depth of understanding of this marvelous mystery—that in Christ, through the gospel, he is a fellow heir with the commonwealth of Israel, a member of His body, and a partaker of the promise. By the working of Your power give him much grace to minister to those in need. Grant him more grace to love and spread the unsearchable riches of Christ, and to bring to light for many what is the plan of the mystery hidden for ages in You who created all things. Through him make known Your manifold wisdom.

Empower him to walk in a manner worthy of the calling to which he has been called, with all humility and gentleness, with patience, bearing with others in love, eager to maintain the unity of the Spirit in the bond of peace. Keep enlarging his heart and mind with the knowledge of Your Son, unto mature manhood, to the measure of the stature of the fullness of Christ, so that he may not be a child, tossed to and fro by the waves and carried about by every wind of doctrine. Guard him from human cunning, from craftiness in deceitful schemes. Enable him to speak the truth in love, to grow up in every way into Him who is the head, into Christ, and to work properly as a member of His body, helping to build it up in love (Ephesians 2 & 3).

ondescending God,

Prevent my husband from walking as the world does, in the futility of their minds. Do not let him live as one darkened in his understanding, hard of heart, callous, or greedy to practice every kind of impurity.

Instead, help him to put off his old self, which is corrupt through deceitful desires. Renew him in the spirit of his mind, and empower him to put on the new self, created after Your likeness in true righteousness and holiness. Make him put away falsehood and speak the truth with his neighbor.

When he is angry keep him from sin; grant him the grace to not let the sun go down on his anger. Let no corrupting talk come out of his mouth, but only such as is good for building up, as fits the occasion, that it may give grace to those who hear. And let him not grieve Your Holy Spirit, by whom he was sealed for the day of redemption. Put all bitterness and wrath and anger and clamor and slander away from him, along with all malice.

Grow us in kindness toward one another, make us tenderhearted, so that we may be always forgiving each other as You forgave us in Christ. Amen (Ephesians 4).

The first reason why prayer leads to fullness of joy is that prayer is the nerve center of our fellowship with Jesus. He is not here physically to see. But in prayer we speak to Him just as though He were. And in the stillness of those sacred times, we listen to His Word and we pour out to Him our longings.
~John Piper

Father of glory,
Assist my husband to be an imitator of You, as Your beloved son. And make him walk in love, as Christ loved us and gave Himself up for us, a fragrant offering and sacrifice to You.

Keep him from any form or appearance of sexual immorality and all impurity or covetousness. And let us both guard our tongues, so that there might not be any filthiness or foolish talk or crude joking, which are out of place, but instead make us abound with thanksgiving.

Guide his feet to walk as a child of light, and enable him to discern what is pleasing to You. Let him take no part in the unfruitful works of darkness, but instead expose them. Open his eyes to look carefully how he walks, not as unwise but as wise, making the best use of the time, because the days are evil. Therefore help him to understand what Your will is.

Fill us with Your Spirit so that we may address one another in psalms and hymns and spiritual songs, singing and making melody to You with all of our heart, giving thanks always and for everything to You in the name of our Lord Jesus Christ. And it is in His name that I come to You with this plea for grace. Amen (Ephesians 5).

Sovereign LORD,

Shall we receive good from You, and shall we not receive evil? Therefore may my husband hold fast to his integrity when calamity comes. Instead of cursing, let him bless You saying, "The LORD gave, and the LORD has taken away; blessed be the name of the LORD." When evil befalls him, let him not charge You with wrong or sin with his lips. And when his suffering is great, enable me to comfort him in wisdom and in righteousness.

May he seek You, and to You may he commit his cause. For You do great things and unsearchable, marvelous things without number: You set on high those who are lowly, and those who mourn are lifted up to safety. You save the needy from the sword of the mouth of the crafty and from the hand of the mighty.

Beloved, behold, your God is faithful when He wounds and shatters you even in your blamelessness. Therefore, do not despise His hard hand of grace, for He binds up, and His hands heal.

Father, deliver my husband from troubles! In famine redeem him from death, and in war from the power of the sword! Hide him from the lash of the tongue, and let him not fear destruction when it comes! (Job 1, 2, 4, 5).

As prayer without faith is but a beating of the air, so trust without prayers [is] but a presumptuous bravado. He that promises to give, and bids us trust his promises, commands us to pray, and expects obedience to his commands. He will give, but not without our asking. ~Thomas Lye

erciful Almighty,
I am but of yesterday and know nothing, for my days on earth are a shadow. Therefore give wisdom to your servant and deal kindly with me that I might live uprightly with the wonderful man You have made for me. Please fill his mouth with laughter, and his lips with shouting. Let those who hate him be clothed with shame, for You are wise in heart and mighty in strength. You command the sun, and it does not rise; You seal up the stars; You alone stretched out the heavens and trampled the waves of the sea; You made the Bear and Orion, the Pleiades and the chambers of the south; You do great things beyond searching out, and marvelous things beyond number.

O how greatly and marvelously You have made my husband! And what a great marvel that You have saved him and kept him with the strength of Your right hand! Praise and glory are due Your name, for You have provided an arbiter between him and Yourself, even the man Jesus Christ, so that You have taken Your rod away from him, and Your dread no longer terrifies him. Therefore may he never loathe his life, or speak in bitterness of soul, for behold, he has an advocate with You, Jesus Christ the righteous (Job 8, 9, 10, I John 2).

Helper of the weak,

I give You praise and thanks for my husband. For Your hands fashioned and made him. You clothed him with skin and flesh, and knit him together with bones and sinews. You have granted him life and steadfast love, and Your care has preserved his spirit.

Therefore please do not destroy him altogether. Remember that You have made him like clay, and do not return him to the dust. Are not his days few? Therefore please bless him, and do not fill him with disgrace. Work wonders *for* him, and not against him.

Oh, that You would speak and open Your lips to him, and that You would tell him the secrets of wisdom! For You are manifold in understanding.

Know, beloved, that God exacts of you less than your guilt deserves, because of Christ. He has taken your guilt upon Himself, therefore be of good cheer and rejoice in the abundant life given you in Him!

Thank You, Father, that because of Your Son, he can lift up his face without blemish; he can be secure and not fear. Let his life be brighter than the noonday, and its darkness like the morning. May he feel secure, because there is hope— hope in Jesus. Let him lie down with none to make him afraid. Amen (Job 10 & 11).

Prayer is the most tangible expression of trust in God.
~Jerry Bridges

reat God,
In whose hand is the life of every living thing and the breath of all mankind, with You are wisdom and might; You have counsel and understanding. Therefore, impart these things to my husband. Lead him with strength and sound wisdom. Let the eyes of his heart feast upon Your splendor. Let them brighten at the sight of Your justice, and with the vision of Your righteousness. For You overthrow the mighty. You uncover the deeps out of darkness and bring deep darkness to light. You make nations great, and You destroy them; You enlarge nations, and lead them away.

When Your majesty terrifies him, and the dread of You falls upon him, let him run to Christ. Even when I am a worthless physician in the day of his calamity, let him cling continually to Christ. And though You slay him, let him hope in You. Do not hide Your face or count him as Your enemy. Please do not frighten him or make him inherit the iniquities of his youth (Job 12 & 13).

Prayer is the acknowledgment of God's sovereignty and of our dependence upon Him to act on our behalf. Prudence is the acknowledgment of our responsibility to use all legitimate means. We must not separate the two. ~Jerry Bridges

ajestic and mighty LORD, Make my husband wise. Impart to him holy insight. And let him not do away with the fear of God, or hinder meditation before You. Keep his iniquity from teaching his mouth, and let him not choose the tongue of the crafty. Open his ears to listen to Your council, so that he does not limit wisdom to himself.

Protect him from the one who is abominable and corrupt, the man who drinks injustice like water. Let not distress and anguish terrify him; may they not prevail against him, for he has not trusted in emptiness, deceiving himself. Do not tear him with Your wrath or hate him, or gnash Your teeth at him. Neither give him up to the ungodly or cast him into the hands of the wicked. Please do not break him apart, or seize him by the neck and dash him to pieces, or set him up as Your target, surrounding him with Your archers. Do not break him with breach upon breach, or run upon him like a warrior. For even though he deserves all these things, spare him because of Christ, for he abides in Him.

O beloved, hope continually in Christ! Look to Him alone for your salvation. Even now, behold, your witness is in heaven, and He who testifies for you is on high. He argues your case with God, as a son of man does with his neighbor.

O Father we offer You praise and thanks for the advocate You have given us in Jesus! (Job 15 & 16).

estorer of the broken in spirit,

Even when my husband makes his bed in darkness, when reproach is cast upon him, when You strip his glory from him, and set darkness upon his paths, when his relatives fail him, and close friends forget him, when his intimate friends abhor him and those whom he loves turn against him, let him hope in Christ. For He lives, and has stood upon the earth, and he shall see Him for himself. His eyes shall behold Him! May he long for that day and not lose heart.

Because he is found in Christ, let his children dance. Let them sing to the tambourine and the lyre and rejoice to the sound of the pipe. May they spend their days in prosperity. Let him receive instruction from Your Son's mouth, and lay up His words in his heart. Cause him to turn always to You so that he will be built up, and remove injustice far from his house.

O beloved, if you lay gold in the dust, and gold of Ophir among the stones of the torrent bed, then the Almighty will be your gold and your precious silver. For then you will delight yourself in the Almighty and lift up your face to God.

When he prays to You, hear him, and make light to shine on his ways. Be exalted! For You deliver him even though he is not innocent, and will grant him cleanness of hands (Job 17, 19, 21, 22).

Whether we like it or not, asking is the rule of the Kingdom.
~Charles Spurgeon

R ighteous Judge,
Thank You that Christ comes even to Your seat and lays the case of my husband before You. He alone is the upright man who can argue on his behalf so that he is acquitted forever by his Judge.

Behold, You know the way that he takes; when You have tried him, let him come out as gold. Make his foot hold fast to Your steps; keep him in Your way and do not let him turn aside. Let him never depart from the commandment of Your lips; may he treasure the words of Your mouth more than his portion of food.

You are unchangeable, and who can turn You back? What You desire, do so in him. Complete what You have appointed for him. Even if You must terrify him and make his heart faint, let him hope in Your steadfast love. May he trust Your hand when thick darkness covers his face. Amen (Job 23).

od of dominion,

Is there any number to Your armies? Upon whom does Your light not arise? Thank You, that because of Christ, my dear husband is in the right before You. Be praised! For he who is born of woman has Him as his purity. His hand pierced the fleeing serpent, and by His spirit he has been made new.

O beloved, adore and fear our God with me. He stretches out the north over the void and hangs the earth on nothing. The pillars of heaven tremble and are astounded at His rebuke. By His power He stilled the sea; by His understanding He shattered Rahab, the terror of the deep. Behold, these are but the outskirts of His ways, and how small a whisper do we hear of Him!

Father, as long as his breath is in him, and Your spirit is in his nostrils, keep his lips from speaking falsehood, and his tongue from uttering deceit. Let him hold fast to Christ's righteousness and not let it go.

Grant him wisdom. For You alone understand the way to it, and know its place. You said, "Behold, the fear of the Lord, that is wisdom, and to turn away from evil is understanding." Therefore increase his fear of You; let him turn away from evil and gain a discerning heart (Job 25-28).

Wise Almighty,

Oh, that You might watch over my husband, making Your lamp to shine upon his head, so that by Your light he may walk through darkness. Let Your friendship be upon our house, and stay always with him.

Keep his children all around him; may his steps be washed with blessing, and cause the rock to pour out for him streams of oil. When the ear hears of him, let it call him blessed, and when the eye sees him, let it approve, because he delivers the poor who cry for help, and the fatherless who have none to help them.

May the blessings of those who are about to perish come upon him, and may he cause the widow's heart to sing for joy. Put righteousness on him and clothe him with it; make his justice like a robe and a turban.

Let him be eyes to the blind, feet to the lame, and father to the needy. Let him search out the cause of even the one whom he does not know. Use him to break the fangs of the unrighteous and make them drop their prey from their teeth (Job 29).

An attitude of acceptance says that we trust God, that He loves us, and knows what is best for us. Acceptance does not mean that we do not pray for physical healing, or for the conception and birth of a little one to our marriage. We should indeed pray for those things, but we should pray in a trusting way. We should realize that, though God can do all things, for infinitely wise and loving reasons, He may not do that which we pray that He will do. How do we know how long to pray? As long as we can pray trustingly, with an attitude of acceptance of His will, we should pray as long as the desire remains.
~Jerry Bridges

od of justice and righteousness, Make my dear husband wise. Fill him with understanding so that men will listen to him and wait and keep silence for his counsel—that they may wait for him as for the rain and open their mouths as for the spring rain.

Let him not despair when his soul is poured out within him, when days of affliction have taken hold of him. When he is cast into the mire, and has become like dust and ashes, let him cry to You for help, and answer him. Even when You seem to have turned cruel to him, may he hope in Your promise; may he wait for Your unfailing love. Let him be a man who weeps for those whose days are hard, and whose soul grieves for the needy.

Assist me to comfort him when evil comes; when he has waited for light, but darkness comes. Grant me wisdom and compassion to bear his turmoil with him; to encourage him when days of affliction come to meet him. Be merciful to him, for he has not walked with falsehood and his foot has not hastened to deceit (Job 30).

ajestic LORD,

Keep my husband from making gold his trust or calling fine gold his confidence. Let him not rejoice only because his wealth is abundant or because his hand has found much. Guard his heart from being secretly enticed to worship the shining splendor of what has been made, for that would be false to You. May he not rejoice at the ruin of the one who hates him, or exult when evil overtakes him. Let not his mouth sin by asking for his life with a curse.

Sanctify him so that he may be able to say that the sojourner has not lodged in the street, that he has opened his doors to the traveler, that he has withheld nothing that the poor desired, and has not caused the eyes of the widow to fail, that he has not left the fatherless hungry. Keep him from concealing his transgressions as others do by hiding iniquity in his bosom.

O beloved, behold, I am toward God as you are; I too was pinched off from a piece of clay. Let us together cling to Christ as our righteousness, for He is pure, without transgression; He is clean, and there is no iniquity in Him (Job 31 & 33).

Intercessory prayer is the purifying bath into which the individual and the fellowship must enter every day.
~Dietrich Bonhoeffer

O God, who is greater than man, Let my husband hope in Christ when his soul draws near the pit, and his life to those who bring death. May his flesh become fresh with youth; let him return to the days of his youthful vigor. When he prays to You, please accept him; may he see Your face with a shout of joy, as You restore to him his righteousness.

O beloved, sing with me before men and say, "I sinned and perverted what was right, and it was not repaid to me. The LORD has redeemed my soul from going down into the pit, and my life shall look upon the light."

Do all these things with him, O Father, to bring back his soul from the pit, that he may be lighted with the light of life.

Listen to me; hear my words and give ear to me. Please teach my husband wisdom. Thank You that he does not drink up scoffing like water, that You have kept him from being a man who travels in company with evildoers or walks with wicked men. May he never say, "It profits a man nothing that he should take delight in God," for such are the words of the wicked (Job 33 & 34).

True, whole prayer is nothing but love. ~St. Augustine

Father, perfect in knowledge, Be praised among the nations! For You have made my husband because You are mighty in strength and understanding. Do not despise him; when he is afflicted please give him his right and keep him alive. Do not withdraw Your eyes from him.

Open his ears to instruction and help him to return from iniquity. May he listen and serve You, and complete his days in prosperity, and his years in pleasantness. Let him not cherish anger as the godless in heart. Deliver him by his affliction and open his ear by adversity. Allure him out of distress into a broad place, and may what is set on his table be full of fatness.

O beloved, behold, God is exalted in His power; who is a teacher like Him? Who has prescribed for Him His way, or who can say, "You have done wrong?" Remember to extol His work, of which men have sung. Behold, God is great, and we know Him not, the number of His years is unsearchable. For He draws up the drops of water; they distill His mist in rain which the skies pour down and drop on mankind abundantly. Can anyone understand the spreading of the clouds, the thunderings of His pavilion? Behold, He scatters His lightning about Him and covers the roots of the sea. For by these He judges peoples; He gives food in abundance. He covers His hands with the lightning and commands it to strike the mark. Its crashing declares His presence; the cattle also declare that He rises (Job 36).

od of thunderous majesty,

Let my husband sing of Your power; when he sees it let his heart tremble and leap out of its place. For You thunder wondrously with Your voice; You do great things that we cannot comprehend. May he bow before You when he beholds the strength of Your word, for to the snow You say, "Fall on the earth," likewise to the downpour, Your mighty downpour. May he worship You with a reverent heart, for by Your breath ice is given, and the broad waters are frozen fast. Let his heart tremble before You in wonder, for You load the thick cloud with moisture; the clouds scatter Your lightning. They turn around and around by Your guidance, to accomplish all that You command them on the face of the habitable world. Whether for correction or for Your land or for love, You cause it to happen.

Hear me, O beloved; stop and consider the wondrous works of God.

LORD, I praise You, for he indeed is one of Your most wondrous works—more amazing than the rain, the lightning, the wind, or the clouds; he shines and declares the glory of Him who is perfect in knowledge.

May he worship You as he looks on the light when it is bright in the skies, when the wind has passed and cleared them. Out of the north comes golden splendor; You are clothed with awesome majesty. Let him praise You as the One great in power, in justice, and abundant in righteousness. Therefore, let him fear You. Amen (Job 37).

ather of my Lord Jesus Christ,
According to Your foreknowledge, in the
sanctification of the Spirit, for obedience to Jesus
Christ and for sprinkling with His blood: may grace and
peace be multiplied to my husband.

Let him bless You, for according to Your great mercy, You
have caused him to be born again to a living hope through the
resurrection of Jesus Christ from the dead, to an inheritance
that is imperishable, undefiled, and unfading, kept in heaven
for him. Thank You that by Your power he is being guarded
through faith for a salvation ready to be revealed in the last
time. Let him rejoice in this. May he rejoice even when it is
necessary that he be grieved for a little while by various trials,
so that the tested genuineness of his faith—more precious
than gold that perishes though it is tested by fire—may be
found to result in praise and glory and honor at the revelation
of Jesus Christ. Though he has not seen Him, let him love
Him all the more. Though he does not now see Him, I praise
You that he believes in Him and rejoices with joy that is
inexpressible and filled with glory, obtaining the outcome of
his faith, the salvation of his soul (I Peter 1).

Prayer does not fit us for the greater work,
prayer is the greater work. ~Oswald Chambers

Father of our living hope, O that You would assist my husband to prepare his mind for action, and to be sober-minded. Let him set his hope fully on the grace that will be brought to him at the revelation of Jesus Christ. As an obedient child, may he not be conformed to the passions of his former ignorance. Instead, as You who called him are holy, make him holy in all his conduct, since it is written, "You shall be holy, for I am holy." And since You are his Father who judges impartially according to his deeds, cause him to conduct himself with fear throughout the time of his exile on this earth, knowing that he was ransomed from the futile ways inherited from his forefathers, not with perishable things such as silver or gold, but with the precious blood of Christ, like that of a lamb without blemish or spot.

O beloved, He was made manifest in the last times for your sake, for through Him you are a believer in God, who raised Him from the dead and gave Him glory, so that your faith and hope are in God.

Enable us, O LORD, to purify our souls by our obedience to the truth for a sincere love, so that we may love one another earnestly from a pure heart, since we have been born again, not of perishable seed but of imperishable, through Your living and abiding word. Praise be to Your name! For this word is the good news that was preached to us. Amen (I Peter 1).

ternal LORD,
By Your mighty Spirit enable my husband to put away all malice and all deceit and hypocrisy and envy and all slander. Make him long for the pure spiritual milk, that by it he may grow up to salvation—since indeed he has tasted that You are good.

Thank You that as he comes to Christ, a living stone rejected by men but in Your sight chosen and precious, he is being built up like a living stone into a spiritual house to be part of a holy priesthood, to offer spiritual sacrifices acceptable to You through Jesus Christ.

I praise You that he is part of Your chosen race, Your royal priesthood, Your holy nation, and a people for Your own possession. And because he is, let him ever proclaim Your excellencies—for You are the God who has called him out of darkness into Your marvelous light. Thank You that although he once was not of a people, now he is of Your people; once he had not received mercy, but now he has received mercy.

Beloved, I urge you as a sojourner and exile to abstain from the passions of the flesh, which wage war against your soul.

Father, keep his conduct among the Gentiles honorable, so that when they speak against him as an evildoer, they may see his good deeds and glorify You on the day of visitation (I Peter 2).

To clasp the hands in prayer is the beginning of an uprising against the disorder of the world. ~Karl Barth

ORD of unbounded mercy,

Help my husband to live as one who is free, not using his freedom as a cover-up for evil, but living as Your bondservant. Let him honor everyone, love the brotherhood, fear You, and honor the governing authorities.

Grant him the grace to endure sorrows while suffering unjustly, being mindful of You. For if he endures when he does good and suffers for it, it is a gracious thing in Your sight.

For to this you have been called, my beloved, because Christ also suffered for you, leaving an example, so that you might follow in His steps. He committed no sin, neither was deceit found in His mouth.

O God, make him like Jesus, so that when he is reviled, he will not revile in return. When he suffers, let him not threaten, but continue entrusting himself to You who judge justly. Thank You that we have a perfect example in Christ Jesus! He himself bore our sins in His body on the tree, that we might die to sin and live to righteousness. May He be exalted! For by His wounds we have been healed. Thank You, that even though he was straying like a sheep, now he has returned to You, the Shepherd and Overseer of his soul. Amen (I Peter 2).

O You who have called us to Your eternal glory in Christ, Please help him to live with me in an understanding way, showing honor to me as the weaker vessel, since I am an heir with him of the grace of life. Help him to do this so that his prayers may not be hindered.

Do not let him repay evil for evil or reviling for reviling, but on the contrary, may he bless, for to this he was called, that he may obtain a blessing. I desire him to love life and see good days, therefore keep his tongue from evil and his lips from speaking deceit; let him turn away from evil and do good; let him seek peace and pursue it. For Your eyes are on the righteous, and Your ears are open to their prayer. But Your face is against those who do evil.

O beloved, even if you should suffer for righteousness' sake, you will be blessed. Rejoice, and have no fear of man, nor be troubled.

Father, may he regard Christ the Lord as holy in his heart, and always be prepared to make a defense to anyone who asks him for a reason for the hope that is in him. Let him do it with gentleness and respect, having a good conscience, so that, when he is slandered, those who revile his good behavior in Christ may be put to shame (I Peter 3).

God delights in the aroma of his own glory
as he smells it in the prayers of his people. ~John Piper

God of all Grace,
If my husband is insulted for the name of Christ, let him take comfort in the truth that he is blessed, because the Spirit of glory and of God rests upon him. If he suffers as a Christian, let him not be ashamed, but let him glorify You in that name. Indeed, when he suffers according to Your will, let him entrust his soul to You—his faithful Creator—while doing good.

Beloved, do not be surprised at the fiery trial when it comes upon you to test you, as though something strange were happening to you. But rejoice insofar as you share Christ's sufferings, that you may also rejoice and be glad when His glory is revealed.

Father, help him to shepherd me, not under compulsion, but eagerly and joyfully, as You would have him; not domineering over me, but being an example. Please clothe us both with humility toward one another, for You oppose the proud but give grace to the humble. We want You. We need Your grace. Humble us, therefore, under Your mighty hand so that at the proper time You may exalt us. We cast our anxieties on You, because You care for us. Make us sober-minded. May we be watchful. Enable us to resist our adversary the devil firm in our faith, and remind us that the same kinds of suffering are being experienced by our brotherhood throughout the world. And when we have suffered a little while, restore, confirm, strengthen, and establish us. To You be the dominion forever and ever. Amen (I Peter 4 & 5).

ompassionate Father,
May grace and peace be multiplied to my husband in the knowledge of You and of Jesus our Lord. Thank You that Your divine power has granted to him all things that pertain to life and godliness, through the knowledge of You who called us to Your own glory and excellence, by which You have granted to him Your precious and very great promises, so that through them he may become a partaker of the divine nature, having escaped from the corruption that is in the world because of sinful desire.

Because of this great blessing, help him to make every effort to supplement his faith with virtue, and virtue with knowledge, and knowledge with self-control, and self-control with steadfastness, and steadfastness with godliness, and godliness with brotherly affection, and brotherly affection with love. Make these qualities his own and let them increase in him, to keep him from being ineffective or unfruitful in the knowledge of our Lord Jesus Christ. May he never be so nearsighted that he is blind, forgetting that he was cleansed from his former sins. Therefore, assist him to be all the more diligent to make his calling and election sure, for if he practices these qualities he will never fall. Please uphold him! And richly provide for him an entrance into the eternal kingdom of our Lord and Savior Jesus Christ. Hasten the coming of His kingdom (II Peter 1).

Prayer is the power that wields the weapon of the Word;
but the Word itself is the weapon by which the nations
will be brought to faith and obedience. ~John Piper

Faithful King,

Make my husband the sort of man who lives a life of holiness and godliness, waiting for and hastening the coming of the day of God, because of which the heavens will be set on fire and dissolved, and the heavenly bodies will melt as they burn. While we wait for a new heavens and a new earth in which righteousness dwells, let him be diligent to be found by You without spot or blemish, and at peace.

Protect him from false teachers that will rise up and secretly bring destructive heresies. Let him not be found among the many who will follow their sensuality and blaspheme the way of truth. Keep him far from the way of the unrighteous, who speak loud boasts of folly and are slaves to corruption. May it never be that after he has escaped the defilements of the world through the knowledge of our Lord and Savior Jesus Christ, he is again entangled in them and overcome! Guard him from such a fate, for his last state would become worse for him than the first.

Therefore, beloved, take care that you are not carried away with the error of lawless people and lose your own stability. But grow in the grace and knowledge of our Lord and Savior Jesus Christ.

Father, may he grow in such grace and knowledge! To You be the glory both now and to the day of eternity. Amen (II Peter 2 & 3).

ather,
Let whatever happens to my husband serve to advance the gospel, so that even his suffering and imprisonment may magnify Christ. May his life be a source of confidence for others in You, that makes them much more bold to speak the word without fear.

Keep him from proclaiming Christ out of envy or rivalry, and instead let him do so from good will and out of love. More than that, let him rejoice in Christ, and in His truth proclaimed. And help him to continue stirring up others for their progress and joy in the faith.

Please let his manner of life be worthy of the gospel of Christ, so that we may stand firm in one spirit, with one mind striving side by side for the faith of the gospel, and not frightened in anything by our opponents. Thank you that it has been granted to us that for the sake of Christ we should not only believe in Him but also suffer for His sake.

Fill us with the joy of being of the same mind, having the same love, being in full accord and of one mind. Keep us from doing anything from rivalry or conceit, but let us in humility count others more significant than ourselves. Let each of us look not only to our own interests, but also to the interests of others, having the very mind of Christ (Philippians 1 & 2).

The true theology is warm, and it steams upward into prayer.
~P.T. Forsyth

Highly exalted God, Please grow my beloved into a man who does all things without grumbling or questioning, that he may be blameless and innocent, a child of God without blemish in the midst of a crooked and twisted generation. Let him shine as a light in the world, holding fast to the word of life, so that in the day of Christ I may be proud that I did not pray in vain or encourage him in vain. Enable me to rejoice and be glad to suffer for his sake—even to pour out my life as a drink offering upon the sacrificial offering of his faith. Likewise let him also be glad and rejoice with me to endure hardship for the name of Christ. Make him genuinely concerned for the welfare of others, seeking not his own interests but those of Jesus Christ.

O beloved, rejoice in the Lord. To say this same thing to you is no trouble to me and is safe for you. Look out for the dogs, look out for the evildoers, look out for those who put confidence in their works.

Father, help him to remain steadfast in worship by Your Spirit, glorying in Christ Jesus, and putting no confidence in the flesh. More than anything, strengthen him to forget what lies behind and strain forward to what lies ahead, and press on toward the goal for the prize of Your upward call in Christ Jesus. Let him also hold true to what he has attained. Amen (Philippians 2 & 3).

reat Savior,
Thank you that my husband's citizenship is in heaven! Therefore let him not set his mind on earthly things, but instead await a Savior, the Lord Jesus Christ, who will transform his lowly body to be like His glorious body, by the power that enables Him even to subject all things to Himself.

Therefore my beloved, whom I love and long for, my joy and crown, stand firm in the Lord. Rejoice in the Lord always; again I will say, Rejoice!

Father, teach him how to be content in every situation. Help him to know how to be brought low, and how to abound. In any and every circumstance show him the secret of facing plenty and hunger, abundance and need. Strengthen him to do all things through You. Please supply every need of his according to Your riches in glory in Christ Jesus. To You, our God and Father, be glory forever and ever! May the grace of the Lord Jesus Christ be with his spirit. Amen (Philippians 3 & 4).

When you encounter trial and suffering, what's the content of your prayer? If yours is primarily a plea for relief from suffering, then please know that this is biblical. It's certainly not unbiblical. We're encouraged by God in Scripture to pray for relief from suffering. But this should never be the exclusive focus of our prayers in those times. ~C.J. Mahaney

Sovereign LORD of Zion,

Let my husband sing aloud and shout! May he rejoice and exult with all his heart. For You have taken away the judgments against him because of Christ. You have cleared away his enemies—death, sin, and Satan. Let him never again fear evil, for You—the King of Israel, the LORD—are near him.

May he not fear, and let not his hands grow weak.

O beloved, the LORD your God is with you, a mighty one who will save; He rejoices over you with gladness; He quiets you by His love; He exults over You with loud singing.

LORD God, when he mourns, please gather him and bring him to Your festival, so that he will no longer suffer reproach. Deal with all his oppressors. Change his shame into praise and renown in all the earth. Restore his fortunes so that You will be renowned and praised among all the peoples of the earth (Zephaniah 3).

Restraining pray'r, we cease to fight;
Pray'r makes the Christian's armour bright.
~William Cowper

od our Savior,

Thank You for Christ Jesus our hope. Watch over my husband and guard him from those who teach any different doctrine, or devote themselves to myths, who promote speculations rather than the good order from You that is by faith. And as you protect him, fill him with the love that issues from a pure heart and a good conscience and a sincere faith. Let him not swerve from these, or wander away into vain discussion.

I thank You, Christ Jesus my Lord, for giving him strength, and because You judged him faithful, appointing him to Your service, though formerly he was so unworthy.

O beloved, rejoice! Remember that you received mercy, and the grace of our Lord overflowed for you with the faith and love that are in Christ Jesus.

I praise You, Father, for showing him mercy, so that in him Jesus Christ might display His perfect patience as an example to those who are to believe in Him for eternal life.

To You, the King of ages, immortal, invisible, the only God, be honor and glory forever and ever! Amen (I Timothy 1).

There is nothing so abnormal, so unworldly, so supernatural, in human life as prayer.... The whole Christian life in so far as it is lived from the Cross and by the Cross is rationally an extravagance. ~P.T. Forsyth

ighty L ORD,
I entrust my husband entirely to Your charge and care, in accordance with Your grace in Christ Jesus toward him. By Your power may he wage the good warfare, holding faith and a good conscience. Let him never make shipwreck of his faith!

Help me to be a woman who prays without anger or quarreling. And continue to give me the wisdom and desire to adorn myself in respectable apparel, with modesty and self-control, not merely with braided hair and gold or pearls or costly attire, but with what is proper for women who profess godliness—with good works. Let me be the kind of woman who learns quietly with all submissiveness.

Protect him from those who depart from the faith by devoting themselves to deceitful spirits and teachings of demons. Let him have nothing to do with irreverent, silly myths. Rather train him for godliness, for while bodily training is of some value, godliness is of value in every way, as it holds promise for the present life and also for the life to come.

May he toil and strive to this end, because he has his hope set on You, the living God (I Timothy 1, 2, 4).

*If we do not abide in prayer, we shall
abide in cursed temptations.* ~John Owen

avior of the weak,
Let my husband set an example for believers in speech, in conduct, in love, in faith, in purity.

Make him find full delight in the sound words of our Lord Jesus Christ and the teaching that accords with godliness. And keep him from an unhealthy craving for controversy and for quarrels about words. Let him instead pursue godliness with contentment, for therein there is great gain.

May he be content that he has food and clothing, and let him not desire to be rich.

O beloved, let us remind each other that those who desire to be rich fall into temptation, into a snare, into many senseless and harmful desires that plunge people into ruin and destruction.

Father, guard us from craving riches! For the love of money is the root of all kinds of evils. Keep us from the fate of those who, through this craving, have wandered away from the faith and pierced themselves with many pangs.

Let our love and craving be for Christ (I Timothy 4 & 6).

For, as for my heart, when I go to pray, I find it so loth to go to God, and when it is with him, so loth to stay with him, that many times I am forced in my Prayers; first to beg God that he would take mine heart, and set it on himself in Christ, and when it is there, that he would keep it there (Psalm 86.11).
~John Bunyan

ather of glory,
As for my husband, let him flee from the desire to be rich and the love of money. Help and enable him to pursue with renewed vigor righteousness, godliness, faith, love, steadfastness, and gentleness. Strengthen him to fight the good fight of the faith, and to take hold of the eternal life to which he was called.

O beloved, I charge you in the presence of God, who gives life to all things, and of Christ Jesus, to keep your conduct unstained and free from reproach until the appearing of our Lord Jesus Christ, which He will display at the proper time—He who is the blessed and only Sovereign, the King of kings and Lord of lords, who alone has immortality, who dwells in unapproachable light, whom no one has ever seen or can see.

To You, O God, be honor and eternal dominion! If You bless us with plenty, let us never become haughty or set our hopes on the uncertainty of riches. Rather cause us to set our hopes on You—the One who richly provides us with everything to enjoy. Help us together to do good, to be rich in good works, to be generous and ready to share, thus storing up treasure for ourselves as a good foundation for the future so that we may take hold of that which is truly life (I Timothy 6).

od and Father,

May grace, mercy, and peace be multiplied to my dearest husband. I thank You as I remember him constantly in my prayers night and day. Thank You for granting me a man who fills me with joy with each new sight of him. Please grow his faith in sincerity. Fan into flame the gifts You have given him, and remind him that You gave us a spirit not of fear but of power and love and self-control.

Therefore let him not be ashamed of the testimony about our Lord, but by Your power cause him to rejoice to share in suffering for the gospel. For You are the one who saved him and called us to a holy calling, not because of his works but because of Your own purpose and grace, which You gave him in Christ Jesus before the ages began. Thank You that He is his Savior, even He who abolished death and brought life and immortality to light through the gospel. Let him not be ashamed to suffer for this gospel, for he knows whom he has believed. Convince him that You are able to guard what has been entrusted to him until that Day.

O beloved, follow the pattern of the sound words that you have heard from the Scriptures, in the faith and love that are in Christ Jesus. By the Holy Spirit who dwells within us, guard the good deposit entrusted to you (II Timothy 1).

It is not well for a man to pray cream and live skim milk.
~Henry Ward Beecher

Father in heaven,
Please strengthen my husband by the grace that is in Christ Jesus, so that he may be able to share in suffering as His good soldier. May he constantly remember Jesus Christ, risen from the dead, the offspring of David. Let him rejoice to endure everything for the sake of the elect, that they also may obtain the salvation that is in Christ Jesus with eternal glory.

O beloved, the saying is trustworthy, for: If we have died with Him, we will also live with Him; if we endure, we will also reign with Him; if we deny Him, He also will deny us; if we are faithless, He remains faithful—for He cannot deny Himself.

O God, remind him of these things. Compel him to do his best to present himself to You as one approved, a worker who has no need to be ashamed, rightly handling the word of truth. May he avoid irreverent babble, for it will lead people into more and more ungodliness, and their talk will spread like gangrene. Thank You that Your firm foundation stands, bearing this seal: "The Lord knows those who are His," and "Let everyone who names the name of the Lord depart from iniquity" (II Timothy 2).

Were it not for the Spirit, none would be able to persevere in prayer. 'A man without the help of the Spirit', John Bunyan once declared, 'cannot so much as pray once; much less, continue...in a sweet praying frame.' It needs to be noted that, for all who persevere in this struggle and discipline of prayer, there are times of exquisite delight when the struggle, and duty slides over into pure joy. ~Michael A. G. Haykin

oly Master,

Let my dear husband cleanse himself from what is dishonorable so that he will be a vessel for honorable use, set apart as holy, useful to You, ready for every good work.

Make him flee youthful passions and pursue righteousness, faith, love, and peace, along with those who call on the Lord from a pure heart. May he have nothing to do with foolish, ignorant controversies, since they breed quarrels. Let him not be quarrelsome but kind to everyone.

Help him to patiently endure evil. Protect him from those who are lovers of self, lovers of money, proud, arrogant, abusive, disobedient to their parents, ungrateful, unholy, heartless, unappeasable, slanderous, without self-control, brutal, not loving good, treacherous, reckless, swollen with conceit, lovers of pleasure rather than lovers of You, having the appearance of godliness, but denying its power. Help him to avoid such people.

Enable him to lead me righteously in his teaching, his conduct, his aim in life, his faith, his patience, his love, his steadfastness, and his persecutions and sufferings.

Indeed, beloved, let me remind you that all who desire to live a godly life in Christ Jesus will be persecuted, while evil people and imposters will go on from bad to worse, deceiving and being deceived.

But as for him, Lord God, may he continue in what he has learned and has firmly believed, becoming more and more acquainted with the sacred writings, which are able to make him wise for salvation through faith in Christ Jesus. Increase his love for Scripture. May what You have breathed out teach him, reprove him, correct him, and train him in righteousness, that he may be competent, equipped for every good work (II Timothy 2 & 3).

My simple exhortation is this: Let us take time this very day to rethink our priorities and how prayer fits in. Make some new resolve. Try some new venture with God. Set a time. Set a place. Choose a portion of Scripture to guide you. Don't be tyrannized by the press of busy days. We all need midcourse corrections. Make this a day of turning to prayer—for the glory of God and for the fullness of your joy.
~John Piper

od and Father of Christ Jesus, who is to judge the living and the dead, May my husband delight in and spread Your word all the more. Make him ready to bear witness to Christ's appearing and His kingdom in season and out of season. Let him reprove, rebuke, and exhort his brothers in Christ with complete patience and teaching.

Guard him from becoming a man who will not endure sound teaching—one who, having itching ears, accumulates for himself teachers to suit his own passions, and turns away from listening to the truth and wanders off into myths. May it never be! Instead, keep him always sober-minded. Enable him to endure suffering, to do the work of an evangelist, and to fulfill the ministry to which You have called him.

O Father, please strengthen him to fight the good fight. Carry him onward to finish the race. Keep him so that he might keep the faith. Effect his heart to love Christ's appearing all the more, so that there may be laid up for him the crown of righteousness, which He, the righteous judge, will award to him on that Day.

May Christ Jesus and His grace be with his spirit. Amen (II Timothy 4).

May God give us a heart and a will to make prayer,
prayer for the exaltation of God and extension of the kingdom,
a daily reality in our lives. ~Michael A. G. Haykin

Appendix A
Books Quoted

Bounds, E.M. *Man of Prayer*
Bridges, Jerry. *Trusting God: Even When Life Hurts*
Brother Lawrence. *The Practice of the Presence of God*
Buttrick, George A. *Prayer*
Carson, D.A. *Call to Spiritual Reformation: Priorities from Paul and His Prayers*
Di Gangi, Marioano. *A Golden Treasury of Puritan Devotions*
Dubay, Thomas. *The Evidential Power of Beauty*
Edwards, Jonathan. *Religious Affections*
Edwards, Jonathan. *The Works of Jonathan Edwards, Vol. 2*
Forsyth, P.T. *The Soul of Prayer*
Grudem, Wayne. *Systematic Theology*
Haykin, Michael. *The God Who Draws Near*
Hosier, Helen. *Jonathan Edwards: The Great Awakener*
Mahaney, C.J. *Humility: True Greatness*
Mason, Mike. *Practicing the Presence of People*
Mason, Mike. *The Gospel According to Job*
Mason, Mike. *The Mystery of Marriage*
Merton, Thomas. *Contemplative Prayer*
Montgomery, L.M. *Emily Climbs*
Montgomery, L.M. *The Story Girl*
Mueller, George. *Autobiography of George Mueller*
Murray, Ian. *Jonathan Edwards: A New Biography*
Owen, John. *The Glory of Christ*
Packer, J.I. *Evangelism and the Sovereignty of God*
Piper, John, and Justin Taylor. *A God Entranced Vision of All Things*
Piper, John. *A Hunger for God*
Piper, John. *Pierced by the Word*
Piper, John. *The Pleasures of God*
Piper, John. *The Roots of Endurance*
Piper, John. *What Jesus Demands from the World*
Spurgeon, Charles. *Lectures to My Students*
Torrey, R.A. *How to Pray*
Tozer, A. W. *God Tells the Man Who Cares*
Ware, Bruce. *God's Greater Glory*
Whitney, Donald. *Spiritual Disciplines for the Christian Life*
Whyte, Alexander. *Lord Teach Us to Pray*

For Further Reading on the Subject of Prayer

Bennett, Arthur. *The Valley of Vision: Puritan Prayers and Devotions*

Calvin, John. *The Institutes of Christian Religion* (Book 3)

Carson, D.A. *Teach Us to Pray: Prayer in the Bible and the World*

Henry, Matthew. *A Method for Prayer*

Hunter, W. Bingham. *The God Who Hears*

Johnstone, Patrick, *Operation World: A day-to-day guide to praying for the world*

Owen, John. *Communion With God*

Palmer, B.M. *Theology of Prayer*

Piper, John. *Desiring God* (Chapter 6)

Piper, John. *When I Don't Desire God: How to Fight for Joy*

Pratt, Jr. Richard L. *Pray With Your Eyes Open*

Spurgeon, Charles. *Prayer and Spiritual Warfare*

Whitney, Donald. *Spiritual Disciplines for the Christian Life*

For Further Reading on the Subject of Marriage

Chapell, Bryan, and Kathy Chapell. *Each for the Other: Marriage As It's Meant to Be*

Greenwood, Glenn, and Latayne C. Scott. *A Marriage Made in Heaven*

Harvey, Dave. *When Sinners Say, "I Do"*

Köstenberger, Andreas J. *God, Marriage, and Family*

Lepine, Bob. *The Christian Husband*

Mahaney, C.J. *Sex, Romance, and the Glory of God: What Every Christian Husband Needs to Know*

Mason, Mike. *The Mystery of Marriage*

Peace, Martha. *The Excellent Wife: A Biblical Perspective*

Piper, John. *This Momentary Marriage*

Riccuci, Gary, and Betsy Riccuci. *Love That Lasts: When Marriage Meets Grace*

Wilson, Douglas. *Reforming Marriage*

Appendix B

Prayers by Biblical Book & Chapter

Also available from Andrew Case:

Water of the Word: Intercession for Her

These books do *not* exist to make money. They exist to edify the Church, spread and deepen a passion for Scripture, and adorn the Gospel. This is why we offer them for free online and sell them for as little as possible. If anyone simply cannot afford to pay for these books, there is a Whatever-You-Can-Afford policy. We will accept whatever you're able to pay—even if it's nothing. It is our joy and delight to give freely what has been freely given to us (Matthew 10:8). We never want to make cost "an obstacle in the way of the gospel of Christ" (I Corinthians 9:12). So if you'd like a copy of a book, but your limited cash-flow prevents it, don't be ashamed! Just contact us and let us know what you'd like, and it will be our pleasure to fill your request.

Phone: 502-802-4383   Email: andrewdcase@gmail.com

Download *Water of the Word* and *Prayers of an Excellent Wife* (as PDF) online for free at: **www.HisMagnificence.com**

4HM3HHEE Use this coupon code to order *Water of the Word* and *Prayers of an Excellent Wife* for only $4.82 per copy. Go to HisMagnificence.com and click on "Books", and there will be a link on that page which will direct you to the store where you can use the coupon code. It does not expire and has no quantity limits.

Upcoming titles from Andrew Case:

Setting Their Hope in GOD:
Biblical Intercession for Your Children
     Anticipated release date: February 2010

Prayers of an Excellent Wife (Spanish)
     Anticipated release date: May 2010

Notes: